MANAGING
to
TEACH

Carol Cummings, Ph.D.

Second Printing March, 1984
Third Printing June, 1985
Fourth Printing April, 1986
Fifth Printing December, 1986

Published by TEACHING INC.
331 - 8th Avenue South
Edmonds, WA 98020

ISBN 0-9614574-0-6

Printed in U.S.A. by
Snohomish Publishing Company
Snohomish, Washington

Table of Contents

SPECIAL THANKS

— to teachers who have shared their management tips
— to Hertha Ledford, Gay Nixon, Allen Neman, Ed Nievaard, and others who let me share video tapes of their proactive classrooms with other teachers
— to Hollyn Howard whose creative mind translated management ideas into cartoons
— to those who perservered on this manuscript; in particular, Britt Nederhood and Doug Kerr
— to Mikel & Jason who gave me a student's perspective on management: "Mom, Mrs. Hawley EXPECTS me to be a good student." "We don't have time to get in trouble in that class!"

CHAPTER 1

Time to Teach

"Who has time to teach? I spend my time managing the classroom, keeping kids in their seats."

Lack of discipline is a frequent complaint among teachers of all grades. Yet, there are some teachers who do not have the discipline problems that plague many others and they produce optimum learning gains. It will be the aim of this book to examine what these effective teachers do that makes the difference.

Why are some teachers more effective regardless of the socio-economic background of students, physical environment of the school, amount of money spent per student or even class size? Typically, these teachers are described in generalities like

high expectations for achievement
accept only the best effort of students
believe that all students can learn
believe in a warm, supportive climate
exhibit positive attitude toward pupils
provide more time on task
have an orderly and structured atmosphere
spend more time in active teaching
use a wide range of instructional strategies

These generalities don't tell the teacher what to do tomorrow morning when thirty kids come barreling through the classroom door. What is needed are specific suggestions of HOW to create the effective classroom. The following chapters will attempt to translate these generalities into practical classroom ideas.

TIME

There is no systematic theory of classroom management (Brophy, 1979). Yet, a synthesis of the research on effec-

1

tive teachers and schools, combined with my own experiences observing hundreds of teachers has led to the focus of this book: managing the classroom through effective use of quantity and quality time.

Time is a variable that has been identified in studies as an essential building block on which to construct a more effective classroom. Effective use of time is seen as a major contributor to the learning process (Berliner, 1979) and classroom management (Corno, 1979). I will argue, however, that a dedication to time on task alone is as inappropriate as concern for quality time alone. When time on task is measured in academic terms alone, we may accomplish high test scores while risking positive attitudes toward subject matter and school. Negative attitudes lead to misbehavior that may ultimately interfere with learning—reversing the initial effect. Conversely, an orientation toward affective and social experiences may be at the expense of time to learn basic skills. A student's low academic self concept may in turn lead to misbehavior and negative attitudes—again, reversing initial efforts.

Only through a balance of quantity and quality use of time will we achieve effective classroom management. Only you, the teacher can make the decision of what that balance should be — how to allocate and fill time effectively.

QUANTITY — AMOUNT OF TIME

Discrepancies between schools of as much as nine hours per week in instructional settings have been found (Goodlad, 1983). These schools were scheduled to convene and dismiss at the same times; yet, it was how that time was spent during the day that led to such a great difference. This loss of nine hours within one week leads to the loss of months of instruction during the school year. The challenge for teachers is to find that extra time to learn.

The goal to provide more time on task for students may be clear, but the means to achieve it are not. Lengthening the school day or school year is not the answer. Extra time can be found within the normal school day.

Often, too much time is spent in preparing for recess or dismissal time, waiting for the teacher to finish "administrivia" at the beginning of the period, or finishing an assignment early and waiting for something else to do. These examples represent potential sources of additional time for learning. Teaching a class a routine for regular activities such as bathroom trips, preparation for lunch, and collecting papers can save precious minutes when compared to repeating elaborate directions.

The time saved in better management leaves more time for quality instruction. The chapters on beginning the school year, teaching a management system, transitions, and using the law of least intervention will provide detailed teacher strategies.

QUALITY OF TIME *

Increasing time on task doesn't guarantee learning or better management. That time can be spent wisely or filled indiscriminately. Teachers can cause learning to occur or simply allow it to happen. Certain teacher activities are more likely to produce learning than others. The amount of time allocated to learning is important, but it is also critical to examine how that time is spent.

Taking time to explain a new concept, monitoring student learning, and providing feedback about the accuracy of response are examples of instructional behaviors related to student learning. In contrast, a teacher spending the same amount of time on independent student seatwork may not produce equivalent achievement.

And, the definition of quality use of time is not the same for all students. The context of the learning environment and the students involved must be considered. Perhaps this is why a "comprehensive 'theory' of classroom management is as elusive as a theory of instruction" (Johnson & Brooks, 1979). The chapters on maintaining accountability through questioning, activating the whole brain, attitudes, cooperative learning, and motivating minority students provide only ideas for quality teaching — NOT prescriptions. The teacher remains the ultimate architect in designing quality time on task!

---

* Teaching Makes a Difference (Cummings, Nelson & Shaw, 1980) also examines quality use of time.

CHAPTER 2

Beginning the School Year

Planning a Management System

The first month, first week, first day, first hour of school are perhaps more important than any other in classroom management. The best managers devote a great deal of time during these first few weeks of school to teaching management expectations (Emmer & Evertson, 1980; Sanford & Evertson, 1980).

Beginning with that important first day, differences emerge between proactive and reactive managers (Evertson & Anderson, 1979; Moskowitz & Hayman, 1976). Proactive managers have name tags ready and waiting for students; greet students at door; introduce students to each other; have easy review materials for them to work on; acquaint class with areas of the room; and teach class appropriate behaviors for socialization into the room. Activities are conducted in the large group to allow for better teacher monitoring. Students aren't given the chance to be off-task.

Reactive managers may have rules posted, but go over them quickly in order to get into academic activities. Very little time is spent in introductions or teaching routines. The expectations are often discussed only after the teacher catches students "misbehaving". They are learned through vicarious punishment. Seatwork given is often too difficult for students and only creates frustration. Many students end up waiting until the teacher is available for individual help. Students may be put into small, unsupervised groups or asked to work for long periods alone before they have been taught the skills of independence.

The lack of organization in these reactive classrooms leads to greater off-task behavior among students. While the amount of off-task behavior may be similar in all classrooms during the first week of school, it in-

"*Rules need to be stressed on the first day of school and periodically during the next few weeks until they are working satisfactorily.*"

Brophy & Putnam, 1979

"*A major management task at the beginning of the year is teaching children the rules and procedures of the classroom.*"

Emmer & Evertson, 1981

creases by 5% in the 2nd and 3rd weeks of school in reactive classrooms (Emmer & Evertson, 1980). This pattern continues to escalate throughout the year. A proactive classroom has very little off-task behavior throughout the year (0.95 to 3.5%) in contrast to other classrooms experiencing far more disorder (7.1 to 18.5%) (Moskowitz & Hayman, 1976). The moral is: every minute of proactive management pays off every day for the rest of the year.

While the differences between proactive and reactive management may be observed during the first day of school — the proactive manager has a great deal of planning to do before that important first day. The teacher becomes an efficiency expert—trying to identify what routines and policies need to be established to allow for maximum teaching/learning time the remainder of the year. The process of building a proactive classroom includes:

IDENTIFYING DESIRED BEHAVIORS
Imagine the ideal classroom. What are the students' work habits? How do you know they are independent learners? These are the behaviors that will have to be taught. This "wish list" might look like this:
THE LEARNER CAN
work without disturbing others
get/return materials to appropriate place
finish/complete work
seek help in an appropriate way
follow routines without reminders
ignore interruptions

respond to teacher's signal (give attention when teacher requires it)

select appropriate activity when finished early

use inside/outside voice appropriately

In addition to these behaviors, consider the times during the day most likely to create headaches or problems. Identify procedures or duties that take time away from teaching. Routines need to be established to keep such administrative headaches to a minimum. This list might include:

attendance taking

bringing notes from home

returning forms

preparation for recess, lunch, dismissal

turning in assignments (location/record keeping)

selecting classroom helpers/monitors

These behaviors and routines are handled in a variety of ways. The key is that they are TAUGHT to the class . . . not told. The following discussion will include both suggestions for managing the routines as well as suggestions for teaching them.

ROUTINES

*Attendance taking and all related administrivia might be handled by the students themselves. A pocket chart with class names could be placed just inside the classroom door. As students enter in the morning, they simply turn their namecard over. They might also record on a slip of paper posted by the pocket chart whether they are buying hot lunch or milk (if such a count is necessary). Some teachers prefer to do this administrivia themselves. If so, they avoid needless waiting while the counts are taken. They begin by giving students directions for a "warm-up" activity first so all can be working. (See Chapter 4 for warm-up ideas.)

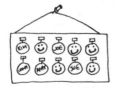

* A box or envelope labeled "notes for the teacher" might be placed on the teacher's desk—a way of organizing and keeping together all correspondence from home. Students routinely place their notes in it. A similar box or envelope might be placed by the door for all correspondence to go home—a good visual cue to eliminate forgetting to send correspondence home. It's not unusual for materials to be sent home to get lost on the teacher's desk.

*Time is lost and confusion evident when teachers haven't established a routine for turning in or collecting work. Passing papers foward each time, with one monitor collecting across the front desks works well. Or, having an "in box" for each subject or period allows students to turn in work individually when finished. This also allows for brief physical exercise before continuing on with the next assignment. Equally important is having a routine to distribute worksheets and corrected papers. Letting students file up by rows or tables to the same location to get work provides another active break during the transition from large group instruction to independent practice. Having a monitor return work while the rest of the class is working independently creates fewer problems than having students waiting (no task defined) while papers are distributed one by one. The waiting almost invites chatting and other off-task behavior.

* Some classrooms cheat students on learning time by preparing for recess, lunch, or dismissal too early. Disorder is frequent during these times. Students may be allowed to return materials, go to coat closet, or wash up "en masse". The traffic jam thus created invites pushing and arguing. A better routine might be to have tables or rows go daily in a particular order. For example, row 1, 2 . . . One classroom prepared for lunch in "thirds": ⅓ washed up; ⅓ got lunches; ⅓ cleaned up working space. The teacher signaled when it was time to rotate to their next activity. Having a clean-up monitor or a buddy system

where buddies check each other frees the teacher to monitor the transition. Using sponge activities (see Chapter 4) while some children are waiting helps keep all productively engaged.

*Disorder is just as likely if the teacher does not allow adequate time for the transition. Some teachers, oblivious of the time, continue talking right up to the bell. The bell then becomes the cue to students to begin scurrying. In the rush, desks may remain messy, materials not put away, traffic jam at the door, and the teacher may not get to deliver last minute directions. A consistent closing routine is needed; perhaps one where the teacher — not the bell — dismisses class.

*Selecting helpers for the week is one way of helping students assume responsibility. Yet, in some rooms this task becomes time consuming and often argumentative. "Who would like to be paper monitor?" Jamie's hand goes up. "O.K., Jamie will be paper monitor." Another student shouts "Jamie had a turn already." "No I didn't", Jamie retorts. And so it goes! In another classroom, students know they'll all have a chance to be a helper and decisions are made without comment. There is an efficient record keeping system built into selection. For example, a rotating wheel can be both a record keeper and an easy way to display job responsibilities. Jobs are pictured or named on the small disk. Student names are on the larger disk. Rotating the disk each week by one name lets you have a new set of helpers. Another technique is to have a pocket chart. A set of 3 x 5 cards with a student name on each is made. A new card is taken from the deck each time responsibilities are assigned. When all cards have been played, a quick shuffle and the process is repeated.

PERIOD	#1	#2
PAPER MONITOR		
BOOK KEEPER		
MESS- ENGER		

*A routine which is a must in every classroom is having a consistent signal to get attention before giving directions or teaching. It's also important to cue or signal students that they need to be ready shortly for a transition (Arlin, 1979). Teachers without signals find themselves in the nagging reminder trap. "Class, may I have all eyes up here please...I'm waiting...I'll only ask one more time . . . I need your attention." How much more pleasant for both class and teacher to give signal only once and have everyone ready to listen. Popular signals include using a bell or flipping the lights. A particularly effective one for primary teachers is the rhythm clap. Teacher claps a four beat pattern (boom, boom, tap, tap, boom); students echo by clapping the pattern. This causes everything to be out of hands and undivided attention on the teacher. Older students seem to enjoy "Give me five". The teacher says "Give me five" while holding up five fingers. The class responds by stopping, perhaps holding "five" up. They have been taught the five attending behaviors of a good listener: eyes on speaker, mouth quiet, facing speaker, hands free, listening. A chart could be posted as a reminder of the five behaviors. One middle school teacher found that squeezing a "rubber ducky" was an effective signal. Perhaps the simplest signal of all is the verbal request, "May I have your attention, please?"

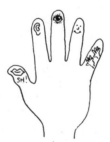

*Pencil sharpening can be a nuisance when students get up while the teacher is trying to teach or when several congregate around the sharpener. Primary teachers often handle this by having one can of sharpened pencils, and one labeled "needs to be sharpened". Students trade one for the other when the need arises. A student monitor sharpens pencils every morning. If students are to sharpen their own,

11

they need to know when they may do it, how many may be at the sharpener at one time, and "how" to do it. It's also helpful to require that two pencils be kept at school.

*A non-verbal record keeping system for bathroom trips keeps track of how many are out at one time. Simply turning a sign over when leaving and returning eliminates the mass exodus at one time.

If it seems that some kids are making unnecessary trips, a sign-out system may be helpful. A class list is placed by the bathroom sign. Students make half an x (/) by their name when leaving; finish the x when returning. If one student has a dozen x's by his name in a short time . . . . it may be time for a short conference! Students also need to know when it is appropriate to leave for the bathroom. Exiting while the teacher is giving directions can only lead to problems.

WILL	X	X			
JOY	X	X	X	X	X
ERIC	X	X			
LISA	X	X	X		
LORI	X	X			
JIM	X	X	X	X	

*If you walked into a classroom while students were on independent seatwork, chances are that you'll see some just sitting...with a hand up . . . . waiting for teacher help. The waiting is not only a loss of learning time, it brews potential trouble. While waiting, why not chat with a neighbor or find something else to do? A signal, other than waving a hand, will allow students to continue working. They can either skip the difficult problem and move on or work on another assignment. A hinged name tag with "help me" written on the back allows students to flip nametag over when help is needed; yet, keeps both hand free to continue working. Or, a "help me" column on the board where kids sign their name and return to work keeps track of the order of those needing help. Or, standing a book on end on the corner of the desk can be a signal that help is needed. One teacher, who prefers to remain at her desk, uses number cards from a bakery. Students take a number; when their number is "called" they go up for help. The teacher can either verbally call out numbers — or can have students keep track of cards replaced, watching for their turn. Again, this is much more effective than having four or five students clustered around the teacher's desk — blocking the rest of the class from the constant monitoring (automatic scanner) of the teacher.

*Some students need to be taught when they can seek the teacher for help—or when the teacher is busy. When the principal or a parent walks in and several students interrupt for help . . . . or, when the teacher is trying to teach a reading group but is continuously interrupted by students . . . . a routine needs to be established. In the primary grades, a stop sign worn around the teacher's neck during the first few weeks of school helps little ones learn to discriminate when the teacher is or isn't busy. A red/green sign hanging in the reading group area serves a similar purpose. An "off duty" sign was observed on one secondary teacher's desk.

*Having a student of the week eliminates the need to choose someone each time an unexpected helper is needed: if the office needs a helper, someone is needed to deliver a message, or even needing an assistant for a new student.

SUMMARY

The suggestions offered above are but a few options teachers have for eliminating the headaches of administrivia in the classroom. These routines eliminate wasted time and misbehavior. The key to success is to identify the management problem and then create a solution to eliminate it! We are only limited by our own resourcefulness and creativity.

While many of the behaviors and routines described thus far are relevant in both elementary and secondary classrooms, the following section will address particular behaviors unique to teachers working with adolescent students.

13

"... the struggle for effective instruction in the inner city junior high school is won or lost at the very beginning of the school year."

Moskowitz & Hayman, 1976

BEGINNING SCHOOL:ADOLESCENTS

Listing the stable characteristics of the young adolescent is a difficult task. Many teachers believe adolescents are unpredictable and physically undescribable. This isn't necessarily so! Adolescents have a fear of being different from everyone else. This leads to a strong need for social security. If we recognize this need, we are in a better position in planning our management system.

Adolescents want to be like their peers; they'll often support a peer over the teacher. They care more about what a peer thinks of them than what the teacher thinks. No longer is the teacher the authority figure whose word is the law. We can apply this knowledge by involving students in establishing rules of conduct for the classroom.

The physical-developmental needs of adolescents should also be considered establishing a management system. Below are several suggestions from a physical developmental checklist for middle schools (Lawrence, 1980).

*Students have regular and frequent opportunities to move about the classroom without disturbing others.

*Vigorous physical activities, including choices of competitive and non-competitive games, are available to every student every day (not just in P.E. classes).

*Students are allowed to work in "strange" postures.

*The school schedule and passing time between classes are planned to avoid build-up of physical tensions.

*Variety and change of pace are provided in classroom activities.

*Lesson plans provide learning activities that engage the whole body.

*School traffic patterns and classroom space are arranged to minimize students' bumping, spilling and dropping objects.

*Students get opportunities for privacy.

Given these unique needs, managing a classroom filled with adolescents is always a challenge. The beginning of the year is as criticial for secondary teachers as for elementary teachers. It's imperative to establish and maintain control immediately. If you lose it, you've lost it forever. It's the job of the adolescent to test the teacher. If they score a "win", they're in the driver's seat. They really don't want to win; they just need to know how far they can go and who will stop them. (Will someone stop me? Can I stop myself?)

Cooperatively involving students in management should eliminate this competitive "them and us" atmosphere and lead to a "we" attitude. Asking students to develop charts listing behaviors they will be responsible for in class is one technique. Another is having expectations planned, but involving students in discussions of the purposes and payoffs for these expectations. Whatever technique is used, consider the following in planning the system.

Setting Routines
The classroom standards of effective and ineffective teachers can be identical: arrive to class on time, bring appropriate materials, gum chewing regulations and grooming and behavior requirements (Emmer & Evertson, 1980). So what is different? First of all, the effective manager makes certain that students have a copy of these rules/expectations. They either have a ditto or have students copy them into a notebook. A list of rules might also be sent home for parents to sign.

HOW TO STAY OUT OF THE DOG HOUSE!

MRS. POLKA'S PROACTIVE MANAGEMENT PROCEDURE*

The success or lack of success that we shall experience during the next few weeks is directly proportional to the number of hours and minutes that we engage ourselves in learning. Thus, those behaviors that are off task or unengaged must be reduced to a minimum.

1. If you drift off task, I will alert you by telling you what you should be doing.
2. If you persist in such behavior after I have alerted you, your name will be written on the board.
3. If you continue to persist, or go off task again, I shall place a check by your name. At this point, I want you to go **quietly** to the office. We need to work it out.
4. If after we have reached an agreement, or understanding, and off task behavior continues, the principal, you and I will meet and your parents will receive a phone call. Again, we want to work it out.
5. If this meeting fails to achieve high on-task behavior, your mom or dad, the principal and I will meet in an attempt to work it out.
6. If this meeting fails to achieve the desired end, you will be placed in isolation for the rest of the mod.

RULES AND PRIVILEGES

1. All students will provide their own **bound** English notebook. This notebook must be brought with you to every class period. Loose paper will not be permitted.
2. All students will provide their own pencil or pen. Your pencils will be sharpened before the late bell rings.
3. If you are absent, it is **your** responsibility to get the notes and assignments the day you return to class.
4. If you are absent the day a test is given or an assignment is due, expect to take the test or hand in the assignment on the day you return to class.
5. All students will hand in assignments on time. The grade will be dropped a letter for every day it is late.
6. All papers must have a proper heading: full name, date, and period. NO ragged edges, please!
7. No student will open windows unless he has permission to do so.
8. You must have a hall pass with you when you leave the room. Use **only** the rest rooms across from Room 313 on this floor.
9. Chewing gum and candy is permitted only if this privilege is not abused.
10. Five extra credit book reports will earn you an additional letter grade.
11. No student will refuse to do an assignment. We never learn anything unless we try! No one will fail as long as a little effort and interest is evident.

*All of the above rules may be altered depending on the circumstance and with special permission. If you are having a problem, please come to talk to me about it. I don't bite! Honest!

*Developed by Audrey Polka, Loveland, Colorado

Consistency is the password for effective management. The teacher who is trying to be one of the students is hesitant to use whatever consequences were identified. Or, if the teachers haven't identified consequences, they ignore the behavior or make up rules on the spot. This leads to inconsistent behavior. It's also the clue to students that they have the upper hand. Students soon learn that the game is to avoid being caught. It's similar to adults. An occasional ticket for speeding doesn't discourage us from that "undesirable behavior". Instead, we install a radar detector to avoid being caught!

Alternatives and consequences must be clearly stated. For example, what happens if a student should be late to class? Every teacher can count on this happening at some time. Ignoring the lateness on one occasion but not the next is the inconsistency we need to eliminate. One teacher taught students to write their name in a designated spot on the chalkboard and then go to their desk. When the teacher has the rest of the class on an independent practice activity, he checks with the tardy student. The effects of such a procedure are to remind the teacher of the tardy student and to allow other students maximum time on task. How much better than listening to a teacher give a fellow student the third degree for being late. The teacher can also determine the consequences for being late depending upon the number of times that particular student has been late in the past.

Every secondary teacher can count on students not bringing materials. Yet, almost every teacher has the requirement that students bring paper, pencil, and book to class. It's the alternatives offered when the "rule" is broken that allow for smoother teaching. Perhaps an extra supply of materials could be kept in a special spot. If the student needs to borrow a pencil or pen, the student's shoe could be left as a deposit. Who could forget to return a pencil with a shoe missing! Or, a stack of IOU slips which the student signs when borrowing supplies and redeems when returning materials works well. One teacher goes through the lockers at the end of every school year to confiscate school supplies left over. He then has a supply to sell students when needed. Having students routinely share a text with their closest neighbor eliminates the wail "I don't have a book!" Covering "loaner" books with fluorescent paper is another protection against having the book "walk out the door". Having a class list where students record when they use a loaner keeps a record of who is abusing the privilege.

Gum chewing is probably the most inconsistently enforced rule across classrooms. Some teachers absolutely forbid it in the classroom while others allow it...as long as it stays in the mouth! It can be a problem within a school when one teacher allows chewing and the next one doesn't. The poor student. It's difficult enough to remember general classroom rules let alone which classes allow or don't allow chewing. Whatever the policy, make it consistent across teachers.

Many routines are necessary in both the elementary and secondary grades. They include:
classroom signal
what to do when entering class
procedures for turning in work/returning work
how to get into groups
group discussion skills
(Elective classes which use special equipment—i.e. science, industrial arts — will have lists unique to that class.)

Like elementary teachers, secondary teachers should spend considerable time in preparation and organization at the beginning of the year. One study found the most effective manager devoted almost one-third of the time during the first five days to teaching rules and procedures (Sanford & Evertson, 1980).

Accountability and Responsibility

Particularly important at the secondary level is the establishment of a clear system for announcing work requirements. The system of accountability should be both explicit and routine. For example, give students a one week schedule of assignments as well as the objectives to be taught.

MATH 7   NEMAN
Week of Nov. 2 - 6

OBJECTIVES — Students will be able to:

Solve division by 2 & 3 digits
Evaluate division expressions
Use order of operations $+$, $-$, X, $\div$
Solve equations with division

	Class Work	✓	Homework	✓	Extra-Basic	Extra-Enrichment
Mon. Nov. 2	p 49 1 - 14		p 49 15 - 20		Lesson 6, Computer	
Tues. Nov. 3	p 50 1 - 12 STAD		p 50 13 - 20			Write 3 story problems using equations from homework
Wed. Nov. 4	p 51 1 - 13		Worksheet		27 A Practice	Hex Puzzle
Thurs. Nov. 5	p 52 - 55 read p 55 1 - 14		p 55 15 - 21			Worksheet: Write expressions
Fri. Nov. 6	Worksheet Solve equations STAD		Study Chap 3 TEST			p 57 1 - 9

*Developed by Allen Neman, Seattle, Washington

Another alternative is to prepare a unit schedule and distribute it at the beginning of each new unit. *

JANUARY 19 - FEBRUARY 17
The Grapes of Wrath

Due to the length of the novel and number of available texts, approximately two class periods per week will be devoted to in-class reading, one class period to writing assignments, one class period to class or small group discussion and one class period to enrichment materials. Each student is encouraged to purchase a personal copy of the novel and a thesaurus. Approximately 25 pages should be read each calendar day to easily complete the novel in the time allotted.

A novel, besides *The Grapes of Wrath*, will not be required this mod. Structured spelling will also be omitted.

The Grapes of Wrath By John Steinbeck

Writing assignments.
Utilize the essay format.

```
┌──────────────────────────┐
│                          │ — Thesis
└──────────────────────────┘

      ┌──────────────────┐
      │                  │
      └──────────────────┘

      ┌──────────────────┐
      │                  │     Support
      └──────────────────┘

      ┌──────────────────┐
      │                  │
      └──────────────────┘

   ┌─────────────────────┐
   │                     │ — Conclusion
   └─────────────────────┘
```

Write a five paragraph essay expressing your opinion; support your thesis with details (facts, situations) from the novel. Direct quotes are encouraged.

Due January 27	"The American Dream" today is much different than "The American Dream" of the 1930s. Or is it? Compare or contrast this concept.
Due February 3	Some families today and the Joads are in similar economic situations. What alternatives do today's families have that were not available to the Joads?
	Possible sources: social studies class, welfare office, lawyers, parents
Due February 7	All novels have a positive or negative effect upon the reader. Describe the effect of *The Grapes of Wrath* on you.
Bonus:	The percentage earned by this question will be averaged into your total grade.
	Choose one:
	1. How does Ma Joad symbolize the strength of the American culture?
	2. Why would this novel be more interesting to you than to another student?

---

* Developed by Audrey Polka, Loveland, Colorado.

Students might be given a form on which they record assignments themselves. This form also includes grading policy as well as provision for periodic parent signatures. Having to handle up to 200 students per day puts the teacher in an awkward position of dispensing rewards and punishment for work. Instead, this helps students monitor their own behavior.

ASSIGNMENT SHEET			Name _____
Subject _____ Teacher _____			Period _____ Qtr. _____

Assignments/Tests	Date Due	Grade		Date		Date
			Student . . .			
_____			Is prepared for class - book, pen, pencil	1 2 3		1 2 3
_____						
_____			Allows others to work without disruption	1 2 3		1 2 3
_____						
_____			Comes to class on time	1 2 3		1 2 3
_____						
_____			Completes assignments on time	1 2 3		1 2 3
_____			1 = Always 2 = Most of the time 3 = Needs to improve			
_____						
_____			Teacher Signature _____			
_____			Parent / Guardian Signature _____			
_____						
_____			Teacher Signature _____			
_____			Parent / Guardian Signature _____			
_____			Extra help is available most days between 2:15 - 2:45			

*Developed by McClure Middle School, Seattle, Washington

Having an "in box" for each class where students deposit homework at the beginning of each class period eliminates a lot of paper shuffling by teachers. Another box for corrected work can be available and a monitor appointed who passes these papers out while the rest of the class is on independent seatwork.

Dealing with absences can be time consuming. One system is to have a "bookkeeper" take class notes daily using carbon paper. This extra set of notes is placed in an "absence box" for students to look at or copy when they return. A buddy system can also foster interdependence. If your buddy is absent, you call that evening and report the day's assignment. The rule observed most often in classrooms is "It is up to the student to get missing assignments." This is sometimes close to impossible. When does the student find the teacher free to discuss missing work? If after school, that could mean six teachers that the student needs to contact. If during class, then other students are deprived of teacher instructional time.

Consistent work requirements across all classes makes it easier to be a successful student. Work requirements can include policy regarding:

heading/form
ink or pencil
one or both sides of paper
policy for late or incomplete assignments
paper type: torn out/spiral/or loose leaf
how to treat errors (erasures?)
policy for typewritten assignments

If teachers can agree to a policy for written work, students are more likely to be successful. These standards will become routine from class to class. One letter might be sent home to parents representative of all teacher expectations.

The following chapter focuses on prioritizing and teaching a classroom management system. The special needs and characteristics of the adolescent should influence these decisions.

CHAPTER 3

Teaching A Management System

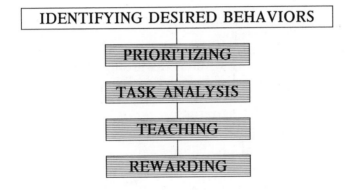

IDENTIFYING DESIRED BEHAVIORS

PRIORITIZING

TASK ANALYSIS

TEACHING

REWARDING

PRIORITIZING

Considerable planning goes into the identification of desired behaviors and routines. The next step is to prioritize the list of desired behaviors. What needs to be taught the first day of school, second, etc. The guiding principle in sequencing which behaviors to teach first is: which are absolutely necessary to maintain a proactive classroom. How can potential misbehavior be eliminated? That is, how can you avoid catching students behaving inappropriately? Below are samples of plan books for the first week of school.

**Routines to teach
the first week of school:**

ELEMENTARY

Monday

signal
   bathroom procedures
   lunch routine
   coat closet/lockers

Tuesday

getting materials
   returning completed work
   lining up
   pencil sharpening
   drinking fountain

Wednesday

fire drill
   working without disturbing others
   choices: if finished early
   how to seek help/teacher busy
   traffic patterns

Thursday

arrival procedure
   classroom helpers
   to/from playground procedures
   inside voice/outside voice

Friday

out of seat policies
   getting to/from groups
   asking questions/raising hands
   end of day routines

SECONDARY

Monday
   signal
   materials needed
   lockers/mapping class routes

Tuesday
   entering classroom routines
   procedures for communicating assignments
   heading papers

Wednesday
   turning in work
   choices: if finished early
   alternatives: if no materials
   procedures if late to class

Thursday
   make-up/absence policy
   routines: bathroom, pencil, library

Friday
   housekeeping/student helpers
   quality of written work
   clean-up routine

TASK ANALYSIS

Each behavior or routine identified needs to be task analyzed before being taught. This skill is not new. We all do it intuitively. Imagine your alarm clock failing to go off. You're 27 minutes off schedule. You'll probably go over a list of things you need to accomplish before the rush begins. "Let's see, I need to shower, dress, and put the garbage out. Thank goodness I took time to grade papers last night." This task analysis of the process considers what has already been accomplished and what's yet to be done. The same process is used in task analyzing routines for the classroom.

For example, a kindergarten teacher or parent may want to analyze the task of getting the kindergartener from home to school on time, using the best route. What needs to be considered? The child. . . .

-knows best route to school

-can recognize specific landmarks along route
-knows to walk on sidewalk
-knows how to cross at corners/lights
-knows to explain to someone if lost (if necessary)
-can state name and address

Specifically, the skill of task analysis involves:
1. brainstorming (what do students need to know/be able to do)
2. sequencing these steps
   a. dependent (certain skills needing to be accomplished before others)
   b. independent (it doesn't matter in which order the skills are taught)

While this may seem like a cumbersome process, reactive management will be the price paid if it's not done. Some teachers believe students should know this "stuff" by junior high—an excuse for not teaching it. It is so much easier to assume that students can "do it" or to simply tell them what they should be able to do. We'll know if we made the wrong assumption about students knowing how to get to school when one gets lost.

I am reminded of my daughter's first day at junior high. She came home in tears. The math teacher had scolded her for being late to class. She was too frightened to tell him she'd gotten lost and couldn't find the room. She had a similar experience this year in high school. She was late to typing because she needed her typing book and didn't realize there wasn't time to go to her locker before class. Teaching students the floor plan of a new school and the best routes between classes could avoid such unpleasant experiences for children.

The junior and senior high have many "firsts" for students: the first time in a large building or multi-building school; first time to have combination lockers; first time to have to pass hourly between classes; first time to have many different teachers, all with different rules and expectations. Each new "experience" for students should be broken down into steps (task analysis), then taught. Below are sample task analyses developed and "field tested" by classroom teachers.

Student will understand locker routine
1. can locate locker
2. know locker combination
3. know how to turn (i.e. left/right/left)
4. know alternative if handle doesn't lift
5. know floor plan of building; shortest route to classes
6. know when best time to go to locker is
7. know to go directly to room if not enough time for locker

Student will seek help properly
1. can identify when teacher is busy
2. will attempt task
3. will consult examples in text
4. knows signal for help (i.e. sign name on board; stand book on desk)
5. will skip problem and work on next problem (or another assignment)

Student will respond to teacher's signal
1. knows what the signal is
2. knows to stop, look, listen when given
3. knows situations when signal will be used

Student knows procedure when finished with work
1. can determine if work "finished" to appropriate degree
2. knows what to do with work
3. knows to check board for list of choices
4. can make choice without disturbing others

Student knows drinking fountain procedures
1. knows when he can get a drink
2. knows sign-out procedure
3. knows where to stand in line
4. understands "space-cushion" idea in line and at fountain (to protect lips and teeth)
5. understands health factor: mouth not on spigot
6. can use appropriate pressure/volume
7. knows what a reasonable time limit is at fountain

Student knows policy for making up work following absence
1. has a buddy; exchanged phone numbers
2. buddy's responsibilities
   -get mimeographed assignment sheet
   -gather books/worksheets needed
3. absentee's responsibilities
   -know time allowed for makeup
   -complete assignments
   -call buddy/get materials
   -place makeup work in designated place

Student will be able to participate in class discussions
1. speak at appropriate times
2. avoid irrelevant comments
3. contribute relevant ideas
4. speak clearly
5. maintain eye contact
6. paraphrase comments of other speakers
7. listen attentively to others
8. avoid inappropriate gestures or posture
9. follow directions of leader or teacher

TEACHING MANAGEMENT LESSONS

Mager (1968) makes the statement that "if telling were the same as teaching, we'd all be so smart we could hardly stand it." This bit of wisdom is equally applicable to classroom management. If telling were the same as teaching, we'd all be so GOOD we could hardly stand it! Teachers take class time to teach subject matter (explain, give examples, check for understanding, provide practice, etc.)—similar time needs to be given to teaching management. One high school teacher explained it this way: "I've always known that the more time I spend on a particular unit, the better my students learn it. I found this year by spending more time teaching management, I've had the best year ever! And, I've had more time the remainder of the year to teach content."

A typical lesson plan for management *or* content might include:
   -mental set (objective and a reason for learning)
   -input (necessary information)

-model (what it looks like)

-guided practice/check for understanding (evidence that students can do it)

-independent practice (students performing task without direct teacher supervision)

MENTAL SET

Let students know what they are about to learn and help them understand why it is important. For example, an industrial arts teacher planned the following set for teaching students to bring materials to class. At the start of class, he walked around the room making comments that he couldn't find his lesson plan book. He asked a number of students if they had seen it. He explained that he needed it for class as he couldn't remember what was planned. He then asked to borrow a sheet of paper and pencil from a student. Glancing to the clock, he commented "Wow! We sure have wasted a lot of time." The class was led into a discussion as to why a person should bring materials to class. He summarized their responses as The Three T's: time, temper, and tomorrow. Time, for learning forever lost. Temper, of others when borrowing and bothering. Tomorrow, because we can't remember everything; notes will help.

Another mental set for a teaching students a signal had students working in small groups brainstorming all the places they've seen a signal used and why it was important. Students listed such things as traffic signals, the coach's whistle in athletics, and the band director's hand motions. After sharing their brainstormed lists, teams were put to work again brainstorming a new list—why a signal might be important in the classroom.

Mental sets for younger students need not be as elaborate. As one teacher put it, "Just teach little ones the behavior, and they'll do it." Older students may look at you and say "Why should I?" Thus, mental set may be the most important part of the lesson plan for the upper grades.

INPUT

Your task analysis is an invaluable tool here. It identifies all of the information students need to have to perform the behavior perfectly. The information is usually given by the teacher through lecture, discussion, or listing the steps on the board. For example, the teacher might explain what the classroom signal will be; that students are to stop, look and listen when hearing the signal, and when they can expect to hear the signal. The information might also be written on the board or overhead projector for all to read.

MODEL

Give the students a chance to see what the behavior will look like—if possible. Two students might be selected to go to the board to solve a problem. While there, the signal might be given while the class watches the two students model what is expected of them. If students are learning how to walk in line without touching, several might demonstrate in front of the room what this would look like. Or, if the class is working on what to do when entering the class, volunteers might role play what they should do. When teaching work requirements, a model of a paper correctly (and incorrectly) headed might be shown. Comparing positive and negative examples gives students practice in discriminating the appropriate behavior and develops better understanding of the concept being taught.

GUIDED PRACTICE/CHECK FOR UNDERSTANDING

Give students a chance to explain their understanding of this behavioral expectation. This lets the teacher know if more explanation is needed. Individual students might be asked to describe the routine/expectation or the entire class might practice it together. For example, if the class is working on correct headings for written work—they could all do one. Or they could all practice lining up . . . getting into groups . . . .or whatever the lesson.

INDEPENDENT PRACTICE

This, of course, is the goal of teaching the management system. When behaviors and routines are established, the classroom runs like clockwork! The key to keeping it running, though, is to "wind it up" occasionally! That is, catch the kids being good! Don't wait for them to forget or ignore a routine (like after the weekend or vacation); instead, continually acknowledge their positive behavior.

REWARDING

Identifying the behaviors wanted in the classroom and teaching them doesn't guarantee they will continue all year long. Rewarding that behavior is necessary. The question is always asked, why reward students for doing what they are supposed to do? Rewards will keep the student "behaving" and lessens the need to punish.

A high school math teacher commented that less than one month after he taught his classes a signal, students were already starting to "forget" what was expected of them when the signal was given. After reflecting upon why this was happening, he concluded he was taking their productive behavior for granted. . . . .and not verbally "thanking" them for it. He inserted a few well-placed "thank yous" in classes the following week and found it worked! They served as a positive reminder of his expectations. This was far more pleasant than the nagging reminders customarily used.

The key to effective use of rewards is that they work only after acceptable behaviors are in place. Hoping to "catch students being good", before teaching a management system, is neither efficient nor effective. It's equivalent to trial and error learning! Inappropriate behavior may occur first, making it necessary for the teacher to react negatively. Or, if the desired behavior happens to occur, verbal reinforcement won't work the same for all students. It may encourage better behavior for some students, while others may feel manipulated or punished in front of their peers. Also, when you "catch one student being good", you may be ignoring bad behavior from another. Frequently ignoring disruptive behavior is an indicator of less effective managers (Emmer & Evertson, 1980).

A reward system that requires tokens or precise tracking of behaviors is not practical for teachers with 30 students—let alone secondary teachers with close to 200. Having to stop a discussion or lecture to give a reward or record a particular student behavior becomes a disruption itself. These behavior modification techniques work best in a special education classroom. This classroom has fewer students who are also working independently.

The challenge, then, is to find effective rewards necessary for maintaining a productive classroom. The big-

"Daddy, guess what?
Just one more check and I
get to see the principal!"

" . . . it is necessary to find out which things are reinforcing for which students. One pupil's perceived reward may be another's perceived punishment."

Popham & Baker, 1973

34

gest difference between effective managers and beginning teachers in inner city schools during the middle of the school year was the use of reinforcing behaviors (Moskowitz & Hayman, 1976).

Reinforcers are probably used more frequently at the elementary level. A list of potential reinforcers identified by high school students (Ware, 1978), in rank order include:
1. opportunity to reach a personal goal
2. school scholarships
3. compliments/encouragement from friends
4. being accepted as a person
5. certificates, medals, ribbons
6. raises/vacations: job related
7. special privileges/responsibilities
8. formal letters of recognition
9. name in the newspaper or over loudspeaker
10. *teacher or employer compliments*

Only a few of these reinforcers are easily within the control of the classroom teacher. In particular, compliments and praise are probably the easiest to use consistently. And, luckily, student behavior is best in classrooms where teachers used an ample amount of praise (Rutter et. al., 1979).

CAUTIONS IN USING PRAISE

Effective praise is dependent upon many variables. It is most powerful in the primary grades. Students in these grades are anxious to please the teacher. Beyond these grades, the risks to using praise increase. As already mentioned, all children do not react the same to praise. It may be more effective with low socio-economic students than high. Likewise, it may cut into students' task persistence and undermine student confidence in their answers (Rowe,1978). Praise may cause students to become less intrinsically motivated to complete assignments (Lepper & Greene, 1978).

To lessen the risks of using praise, Brophy (1981) has developed a set of guidelines to consider in designing effective praise. (To be considered praise by Brophy, teacher reaction to student behavior is more elaborate than necessary.) The suggestions include:

Make praise contingent upon a particular behavior —not delivered randomly after student answers (correct or incorrect) or for no particular reason.

Specify the desired behavior. "You did a great job of coming in quietly and getting to work today. Thank you." Global comments ("Nice job today") don't tell the students what is expected of them.

Show spontaneity and variety. Habitual reactions like "Fine", "OK", "Good" don't focus on the individual. Kids soon tune out to stock phrases. They function more as punctuation marks to student comments!

Consider giving individual praise privately with older children to avoid the teacher pet syndrome or embarrassment. The old "hit and run" technique works well with students who have a difficult time receiving praise—deliver it and move on quickly, not waiting for a reaction!

Verbal must match non-verbal. The old saying "Your actions speak louder than words" is particularly true here. A smile, nod, or wink—not a flat tone and deadpan expression—communicate sincerity. (Brophy believes that the variables of teacher warmth and personal interest may be more important than praise alone.)

Focus students on their own effort and ability. "You really put extra effort into cleaning up the art center. The paint table is spotless. Thank you!"

Avoid teacher pleasing "I really like . . ."; or *comparing the student with others:* "Sara, you're almost up with Clara. Good."

Avoid linking a student's success with luck or an easy task. "You did fine, Zoey. It must have been an easy assignment."

The goal is to help students develop intrinsic satisfaction for their productive behavior. Additional examples include:

"You must feel pretty good about how quietly you came in today."

"Your heading is excellent. What do you think is best about it?"

"The substitute reported this class was really well behaved yesterday. What things did you do that you are especially proud of?"

"Give a silent cheer for your cooperative groups today. Let's list the things you did so well . . . " (Students raise their clenched fist several times in air for silent cheer.)

"Class, take your right hand and place it on your left shoulder. Now lift it up and down several times. Great. Now, what did I have you do that for?" Students in this class were grinning, guessed they must have done something well to deserve a pat on the back. The teacher then put a list of three routines he'd taught the class earlier on the overhead and thanked them for their efforts. (This was observed in a high school typing class!)

Get students to THINK about their productive behavior, not just hear the teacher mention it.

WHEN TO PRAISE

After teaching a routine or expectation, reinforce that behavior as you observe its occurrence. Then distribute these "positive acknowledgements" across the ENTIRE school year. One high school teacher writes reminders to himself in his plan book: "Reinforce class for. . . ."

In addition to distributing reinforcers, there are definite times throughout the school year that students will need to be "reminded" of expectations: before and after holidays and vacations; changes in routines; assemblies; etc.

Don't forget: You can catch more flies with honey than you can with vinegar!

SCHOOL WIDE ROUTINES/EXPECTATIONS

It may be necessary to work on a routine on a school-wide basis: bus standards, lunchroom behavior, playground behavior, assembly standards, hall conduct, etc. The same steps of task analysis, teaching the behavior, and "catching kids being good" still apply.

Many elementary teachers have found that playground

problems find their way into the classroom. Students don't want to go out to recess . . . . some come back in tears . . . . some still fighting as they walk back into class. One school partly solved the problem by identifying the kinds of things students need to know to be successful at recess time, then divided the responsibility for teaching these among the teachers. Their task analysis for playground behavior looked like this:

Does the learner know:
1. perimeter of playground
2. how to line up at signal
3. how to retrieve ball if it leaves playground
4. how to play basic games:
    four square
    softball
    slide
    jump rope
5. basic etiquette (i.e. don't walk through a game others are playing)
6. safety rules

Teachers in the building set aside a time in the afternoons during September to teach their assigned task. Classes rotate to a new lesson each day—but each teacher has only one lesson to prepare. If Ms. Sanders teaches her class four square on Monday, her class rotates to another teacher for a different lesson on Tuesday, etc. Playground supervisors in this building have been particularly aided by this because all students in the school are "playing by the same set of rules". They're not faced with "This is how we play four square in OUR room!" when arguments break out.

The job of teaching lunchroom procedures has been tackled by many principals. One principal decided to convert her lunchroom into a "cafeteria". Tables were moved apart as at a cafe, instead of being placed in long formidable rows. Room numbers were assigned to sets of tables—so each room was responsible for their own section. Each month centerpieces are placed on the tables: pumpkins in October; leaves in November, boughs of holly in December, etc. Quiet classical music is played during lunch. The task analysis for student behaviors included:

1. what to bring with you to cafeteria
2. lining up for hot lunch/milk
3. selecting hot lunch items
4. carrying trays
5. traffic pattern to reach table
6. table manners
7. voice level
8. clean up procedures/standards
9. how to exit
10. supervisor's signal for attention

The principal took each room in the building, one by one, through the lesson in the new "cafeteria".

A junior high principal tackled school wide behaviors by having teachers rank order a list of behaviors they thought most important for school wide acceptance. The top three for teachers at his building were: respond to teacher signal; work on assignment at beginning of period (warm-up activity); and hall conduct. The staff met the day before school began and analyzed these behaviors. They developed a group lesson plan. On the first day of school each first period teacher taught lesson #1 (signal). As students progressed from class to class the remainder of the day, they only had to be told what the new teacher's signal would be. The second day all first period teachers taught "warm-up" lessons. Students found an assignment on the board in each class they went to that day (and every succeeding day!) One student was overheard commmmenting "What'd you teachers do...get together and decide to really organize this building?"

Similar building wide behavior plans can be developed and taught for other areas. At a staff meeting, teachers in one elementary school agreed that entering the building before school and at recesses was creating problems. They decided upon teaching the following:

When entering building:

1. walk to door
2. wait in class line until teacher arrives
3. use quiet voice

4. hand on rail for stairs
5. one stair at a time

Each teacher posted the policy in their room, held a class discussion as to why this was important, and role played the behavior with the class. At the next staff meeting, teachers met to work out the "bugs" to their efforts.

The consistency in behavioral expectations throughout a school is another step toward promoting that "orderly school climate" characteristic of effective schools (Shoemaker & Fraser, 1981). Principals and district administrators are key actors in this process. Their expectations and efforts contribute to an orderly school climate which facilitates learning. I had the opportunity to visit a superintendent's office in Detroit and saw high expectations in action. On one wall was the sign, "We CAN achieve what we believe." Beside the sign were standardized test scores for the past five years through the ninth grade. The stair-step graph showed a steady increase across each grade every year. Her efforts to foster a positive school climate and effective instruction were paying off.

DON'T FORGET THE SUBSTITUTE
A class may be running like clockwork. Routines established. Maximum time on task. Then, the teacher gets sick. Within minutes it is possible for that ideal class to forget (or, ignore!) that management system. Anticipating this, the proactive teacher should supply the substitute with as much information about the management system as possible. When the sub hears those familiar refrains "That's not the way our teacher does it," or, "We always get to do this in our class!", there is "something" to refer to. Below is an example of a substitute form used successfully at one elementary school (in Bothell, Washington).

Dear Substitute:

The information in this folder has been prepared to provide you with a good deal of general information about my class. Specific daily lesson plans will be furnished in addition to this. I hope the material is useful and that you have a good day with my group.

When you have finished the day, please complete the enclosed evaluation sheet and return to the office with this folder.

Sincerely,

Teacher _____   Room _____ Grade _____

Home Phone Number _____

Inside you will find:
Schedules (classroom and building)
Emergency procedures
Classroom rules
Building and playground rules
Attendance forms
Class list
Time schedule
Seating chart (if name tags not used)

TIME SCHEDULE

Doors open at _____

School begins at _____

Recess is scheduled for _____

Lunch time is _____

Noon recess is scheduled for _____

Dismissal time is _____

My signal for getting student attention is:

_____

All students should STOP, LOOK, LISTEN.

41

Dependable Students

_____

_____

_____

_____

_____

_____

Possible Disciplinary Concerns

_____

_____

_____

_____

_____

Health Concerns

_____

_____

_____

_____

_____

Extra Duties

Check daily bulletin for any recess,
bus,   or   hall   duty.

Out of Classroom Activities

Speed reading, music, patrol, A.V.,
library, staff, kitchen, etc.

Name   Activity   Time

_____

_____

_____

_____

_____

_____

_____

_____

_____

_____

_____

Student Classroom Responsibilities

End of day room pick-up, chairs,
etc.:

_____

_____

_____

_____

_____

Fire Drills

Continuous horn: Take class to

_____

(chart enclosed). Make sure doors
and windows are closed and lights
turned off.

_____

Civil Defense Drills

Intermittent horn: Prop doors open,
pull drapes, and have children get
under their desks with arms covering heads.

Lunch

Time and procedures: _____

_____

_____

_____

_____

Lunch charge money is located:

_____

Discipline

Students are expected to follow
building rules as well as reasonable
requests from adults. Specific room
rules are:

_____

_____

_____

_____

_____

Consequences to Disruptive Behavior

_____

_____

Extra Time

When children have free time (after
completing assignments early) they
are to:

_____

_____

Extra ditto work is located in a
folder so marked in my bottom file
cabinet drawer.

Out of Classroom
Activities Schedule

P.E. _____

_____

Music _____

_____

Library _____

_____

Special Directions

My teachers' manual will be found:

_____

_____

Dismissal Procedures Are _____

_____

_____

_____

Restroom Procedures

_____

_____

_____

DAILY ROUTINE

Correspondence from home _____

_____

Restroom _____

_____

Drinking fountain _____

_____

Pencil sharpener _____

_____

Talk among students _____

_____

Passing out books/supplies _____

_____

Out-of-seat policies _____

_____

Want to do when finished w/work _____

_____

Where to turn in completed work _____

_____

Failure to bring materials (pencil, paper, textbook) _____

_____

Dismissal Procedures are _____

_____

CHAPTER 4
Transitions: Eliminating Dead Time

A teacher may have a commitment to creating maximum time on task—spending the larger proportion of class time in instruction. Yet, there are times during the day when even the most committed and best planned teachers are faced with *dead time.* Dead time can occur:

> at the beginning of the period or day
> between reading groups
> before/after recess & lunch
> at the end of the day
> before/after any transition (i.e.assembly, special class)
> when a student finishes seatwork early

During dead time students are waiting. . . . .for the next activity to begin. Students are not engaged in learning and the potential for discipline problems increases. Arlin (1979) found that off-task behavior during transition time was almost twice that of regular classroom time. The risk of disruption and inappropriate behavior is greatest. Lower ability children—who are often our behavior problems—have a higher proportion of academic dead time (Evertson, 1980).

The best managers have activities to eliminate dead time (Emmer, & Evertson, 1980). To prevent both loss of instructional time and discipline problems, this chapter will present short filler activities that require little or no preparation or materials. Evertson (1980) calls these brief activities "warm-ups" when they occur at the beginning of the period and allow the teacher to attend to procedural and housekeeping duties. Madeline Hunter (1973) refers to them as "sponge" activities as they sop up potentially wasted time. These activities should not be viewed as simply fillers. They deserve a definite instructional purpose: either as a practice activity of material previously learned or a mental set for a new lesson. They may be either teacher led or independent activities for students. Independent sponges are necessary when the teacher has administrivia to attend to. It is critical, though, that the activity be easy enough for the student to accomplish without teacher assistance.

WARM UPS (independent work)

Students need only a few minutes to accomplish these activities. They can be written on a "think pad" or scratch paper. Some sort of accountability system, though, is necessary to insure that students do the warm up. This may be something as simple as the teacher walking around monitoring the work to the time consuming task of collecting them. Some teachers have students keep these warm-ups in their notebook with the promise that future tests will include questions from them. The following warm ups are appropriate for any subject:

1. Write down three questions about _____. Be ready to quiz another person.

2. Taking no more than 3 minutes, brainstorm all you know about _____.

3. Find the glossary. Look up the word _____. Write the definition using different words.

4. Scan Chapter for terms in **bold print** or *italics*. Make two lists, 3 terms you know and 3 terms you don't know. Use your glossary, rewrite the definition for unknown terms in your own words.

5. One term does not belong. Cross it out. Propose a title for the remaining items.

6. Put these terms into two groups and suggest a title for each group.

7. Scan Chapter ____. Outline the major topics and subtopics.

8. Describe at least one way that learning about _____ can help you in the future.

The above activities may be used over and over again—inserting new chapters, concepts, or vocabulary. Having them permanently written on a transparency allows you to plan your warm-ups for the week in advance—just placing a different one up each day. Following is an example from social studies. The class was studying the Westward Movement.

ONE TERM DOES NOT BELONG. CROSS IT OUT.
PROPOSE A TITLE FOR THE REMAINING ITEMS.
California, Texas, Pacific Northwest, Southwest

PUT THESE TERMS INTO TWO GROUPS.
SUGGEST A TITLE FOR EACH GROUP.
James Polk, John C. Fremont,
Andrew Johnson, Sam Houston, John Q. Adams

WRITE DOWN THREE QUESTIONS ABOUT THE
"MOVING FRONTIER". BE READY TO
QUIZ ANOTHER PERSON.

TAKING NO MORE THAN 3 MINUTES,
BRAINSTORM ALL YOU KNOW
ABOUT OREGON'S HISTORY.

Primary teachers need warm-up activities that don't require as much reading and writing. Kindergarten and first-grade teachers might have a ball of clay in each student's desk. Each day when the kids are waiting to begin, they might see what the teacher has written or drawn on the chalkboard and reproduce it with clay at their desk. This could be letters or numbers or simple words. This could be reading practice by asking students to make/construct whatever word is written (i.e. cat, house). Individual chalkboards can be used in a variety of ways. Boardwork can tell students to practice making a letter ten times and circle their best three; give simple math problems; or have a list of words to put in alphabetical order. A counting pattern might be on the board with directions for students to continue it as long as they can:

1, 2, 3 . . . . or,
2, 4, 6, 8 . . . . .or,
34, 33, 32, 31, 30 . . . .

SPONGES (teacher led)

The following teacher led sponge activities may have either the teacher call randomly on students or require that students raise their hand and wait to be called upon. They can be used while standing in line, waiting for dismissal, or whenever the need to eliminate dead time or waiting arises.

1. *CATEGORIES:* When the teacher is just beginning sponge activities with students, name the category first to make it easier for students to have a successful first experience. Students then give examples that fit the identified category. "Class, let's play categories. Today's category will be 'presidents'. I'll start it out with Eisenhower." Once the class is used to this activity, the teacher might simply start out with examples and not name the category:

i.e. "hat, bed, horse,. . . . raise your hand when you can give another example!" (category is nouns)
i.e. "hit, mat, flat. . . . ." (ending consonant sound of t)
i.e. "meter, liter, gram. . . . ." (metric terms)

By not naming the category first, students have to look for similarities and differences in the examples given to identify what attribute they have in common. This requires more complex thinking and is great for concept development.

2. *YOU CAN HAVE. . . . BUT YOU CAN'T HAVE . . .*
This requires students to give both a positive and negative example of a concept. Again, the teacher may want to begin by naming the concept first. When students are accustomed to the game, give example and non-example only. This will require more complex thinking from students and foster concept development.

48

i.e. "The concept is authors. You can have Shakespeare but you can't have Ronald Reagan. Who can give me another?"

i.e. "You can have a dog but you can't have a snake. You can have a whale but you can't have a salmon. Who thinks they can give me another?" (concept is warm blooded animals)

i.e. "You can have Fort Worth but you can't have Texas. You can have Lansing, but you can't have Michigan." (city but not its state)

The above two sponges can be played at any grade level and with any subject matter. Following are sponges grouped according to subject matter.

MATHEMATICS

1. *SILENT MATH* This is a favorite of most teachers. Every student answers with a nonverbal finger signal for every problem given. Students are taught the nonverbal signals for adding (crossed pointer fingers), subtracting (horizontal pointer finger), multiplying (forearms crossed in an X), and dividing (one hand flat and horizontal while the other has pointer and thumb placed above and below as dots). The teacher gives the class a problem (i.e. 5 + 3), then nods for the class to signal the answer back with their fingers. Students are to place finger answer against their chest so answers aren't likely to be copied. Secondary students enjoy the challenge of a multi-step problem leading into the hundreds: $10 \times 10 \times 7 \div 5 \div 10 - 8$. The teacher must be sure the final answer will be 10 or less. This type of math practice is more relevant to how we compute as adults than having problems on a worksheet.

2. *ALSO KNOWN AS* This encourages students to identify other mathematical expressions that have the same value as the one given by the teacher: "Also known as 10 x 5" Students may answer "Also known as 100 divided by 2"; "Also known as 10 + 10 + 30", etc. Practice in equivalent units of measurement can be used: "Also known as three feet." Fractional equivalents can be used: "Also known as 3/4."

3. *CHAINING* Teacher begins a pattern of numbers, which students continue adding to when they think they

know the pattern: "19, 25, 23, 29. . . . who can give me the next number?" (pattern is plus 6, minus 2) "52, 54, 53 1/2, 55 1/2, 55...who has the next number?" (pattern is plus 2, minus 1/2)

4. *BACKTRACKING* This game of mental math computation can have all the students signal the answer if the teacher stays below ten. "I am thinking of a number. I multiply it by three and add four. The number is now ten. What number was I thinking of? Signal with your fingers." (2) "I am thinking of a number. I divide it by 2; multiply by 10; divide by 10 and end up with 5. Signal my original number." (10) Many students are visually oriented and will want to jot down the operations on scratch paper—the teacher might need to, too!

5. *WHAT'S THE QUESTION* To help students become aware of the variety of questions that can be asked in story problems, the teacher gives "the facts", the students see how many questions they can design. "Twelve cats and fifteen dogs; ask a question." Students might answer: How many animals all together? How many fewer cats were there? How many more dogs? How many dog and cat pairs could be formed? An alternative version of the sponge can have students respond in unison with the answer to each question. This activity is also a good written warm up activity.

On the board:
$13.95
$15.00
(a) Write a story problem using the above
(b) Write the equation to solve it
(c) Solve your equation

6. *TELEPHONE NUMBER* The number of things a teacher can have students do with their own phone number is endless! How many math problems can you make? Write a story problem using all of the digits. Add the digits; who has the largest sum? Who can form the largest number by rearranging their digits? Multiply each digit by the next. Who has the largest/smallest answer? In groups of 4, put your numbers in numerical order. The imaginative teacher can probably design weeks of sponges just by having students use their phone number! Scratch paper is needed.

7. *PROBLEM MAKER*   Teacher gives students a set of numbers and symbols for operations: 8, 12, 7, 14, 6, 5; $+$, $-$, $=$. Students are asked to see how many different equations they can make; or, what the longest number sentence might be; or, how many equations can be made with the same answer.

8. *STORY PROBLEM FUN*   Story problems can be practiced in small "chunks". One problem can be placed on the board for the week. Each day the sponge can be to answer a different question about that problem: write it in your own words; label the missing fact; what are the irrelevant facts; what are the relevant facts; make a diagram or picture of the problem; write the equation needed to solve the problem. A reverse of this sponge would be to have students write a story leading to a given equation: "Write a story leading to this equation:
$$43 - 18 + 7 = \underline{\hspace{2cm}}$$"
The National Council of Teachers of Mathematics recommends that problem solving be the focus of school mathematics in the 1980s (The National Council of Teachers of Mathematics, Inc., 1980).

LANGUAGE ARTS
1. *FORTUNATELY/UNFORTUNATELY*   This is a great activity to encourage building related sentences (critical to paragraph writing) and creative ideas. The teacher begins "Fortunately, today is Friday. Unfortunately, the forecast is rain for the weekend. Who can add the next sentence?" A student begins "Fortunately. . . . " and continues the story line. Or, the teacher might begin with fantasy: "Fortunately I was born an Egyptian princess. Unfortunately, my family was exiled to Cuba. . . . " The story can continue until the "wait time" is filled.

2. *PAIRS*   The teacher initiates the activity giving pairs of words—they can be all opposites, synonyms, homonyms, same vowel sounds, parts of speech, etc. Students must figure out what they have in common and give another pair. "Yes-no; up-down; hot-cold; who can give another pair?" (opposites) "Sat-stamp; ship-pin; gate-play" (matching vowel sounds); "of-in; house-boat; run-jump; slowly-tightly"(matching parts of speech)

3. *SPELLING* A list of words is begun, but each new word in the list begins with a particular letter from the previous word. It may begin with the last letter of the previous word, second from the last letter, etc.

"Slip, pen, no, over, red . . . "

"Crate, apple, place, anger, goose . . . "

Encourage students to visualize the spelling of words to figure the pattern out. The game can be altered by having all words fit the same category: hat, thumb, baby, yard, etc. (All are nouns plus each begins with the last letter of previous word.)

4. *MIXMASTER* To encourage students to speak in complete sentences as well as look for relationships between concepts, the teacher selects any two words and calls out mixmaster. Students must use those two words in a sentence. "Liter/quart — mixmaster" One student may answer "The liter and quart are units of measurement." Another may say "One liter is a couple of ounces larger than a quart." This sponge can be played with volunteers, round robin around the classroom, or with students calling out the name of the next person to answer ("Mixmaster, John").

SOCIAL STUDIES/SCIENCE

1. *DETECTIVE* A form of the game of twenty questions. Teacher gives clue and how many guesses will be allowed. Questions may be answered by a yes or a no. "I'm thinking of a state in the United States. Twelve guesses." "I'm thinking of a planet. Four guesses." "I'm thinking of a bone. Ten guesses." "I'm thinking of the current leader of a country." By challenging students to a limited number of guesses they are more likely to strategize in asking questions.

2. *MIXMASTER* Teacher names two concepts that are related in some way: "Cell/protoplasm — mixmaster." Students are to combine them into one sentence. ("Protoplasm is the living material found in a cell.") "Canoe/Indians — mixmaster" ("The canoe was the chief means of transportation for coastal Indians.") Several sentences might be solicited for every pair of concepts. This game allows able students to elaborate on the relationship be-

tween ideas and the less able to demonstrate recognition of the terms.

3. *ENDLESS CHAIN* Teacher names a broad topic (plants; rivers; inventors; books). Students add to the list with an example from that category that begins with last letter of previous word. "Let's make an endless chain with cities." (Seattle, East Lansing, Grandview, Wichita, etc.)

4. *MIND BENDER* This is a good activity to reinforce listening and memory skills. Teacher names a topic. Each student gives one sentence about the topic BUT must repeat each previous sentence given. "Let's see how far around the room we can get playing Mind Bender. Our topic will be Abe Lincoln." First child might say: "Lincoln wrote the Gettysburg Address." Next student must repeat first sentence, then add another (i.e. Lincoln wrote the Gettysburg Address. Lincoln was a U.S. President.)

TICKET OUT THE DOOR

This is a sponge to use when there are a few extra minutes at the end of the day or class period. It promotes meaningful processing of what students learned during the day. It can be written on a scrap of paper and handed to the teacher on the way out the door. Occasionally teachers suggest students take them home. Questions students might be asked to respond to, as a "ticket out the door" might be:

-List one thing you learned today.

-When you get home, what will you tell your parents you learned today?

-Write one reason why today's lesson may help you in the future.

-List as many occupations as you can that need the skills we practiced today.

-Describe one thing you felt good about today.

-Or, any other question that is related to the content taught or feelings about the day.

FINISHING WORK EARLY

This is probably the most frequent cause of dead time in classrooms. Yet, most teachers respond by saying that they've told their students to read or finish other homework if they have extra time. Students hear the same admonition year after year after year; and, at the secondary level, class after class. Two techniques that seem to be more effective than the traditional approach are "Choices" and "Centers".

CHOICES   A list of different activities that students may choose from is given. This list is changed weekly. One thing that is NOT on the list is another worksheet or more of the same type of work just finished. One of the choices might be a challenge activity. A knowledge of Bloom's Taxonomy can help the teacher design activities that are related to the previous seatwork but more cognitively complex. For example, if students finish reading and answering chapter questions on World War II, they might find these to chose from:

"Make a choice: 1. Jot down several things you would have done differently if you were President at the beginning of World War II. 2. Make a crossword puzzle using information from the chapter. I will select some to use in class. (This is assuming students have been taught how to make a crossword puzzle.) 3. Go to the library and select a book to read on the war. 4. Read your own library book."

The variety of activities provided is more likely to spark the interest of early finishers. The crossword puzzles prepared by students might even be a "choice" activity another day.

CENTERS   Centers are most frequently used in the primary grades. Their use, however, is encouraged for all grades. Several areas in the room are set up with a variety of activities that function as sponges. Examples of activities found in centers might be:

-story-starter corner: cards with unfinished sentences (i.e. The thing that bugs me most. . . . .; One thing I like is. . . . .; If I were the teacher in this room, I would. . . .) Writing materials are supplied and students are encouraged to write as much as they please. Some rooms have a bulletin board adjacent to the center where stories can be displayed immediately (if the student so chooses). Several students can work at this center.

-tape recorder center: student selects a favorite story and reads it into the tape recorder. The student can play the

story back. This is a good activity to promote reading with expression.

-typing corner: a typewriter is available for students to type a story or poem they have written or a favorite one from a book.

-create a story corner: a pocket chart with pockets for characters, place, and problems. Students draw a card from each pocket and create a story. Again, an adjacent bulletin board is handy for students to post finished stories.

-greeting card center: a variety of art materials available for students to make their own for any birthdays coming up, sick friends or relatives, or someone they'd like to say "hello" to. One teacher had the caption "Want to write a note to a friend during class with teacher permission?"

-letter writing corner: a list of famous people and their addresses is posted as well as a model of a friendly letter. Colored ditto paper with lines encourages students to write. A stack of magazines that have free materials to write for as well as a model of a formal business letter can encourage adolescents.

-travel center: Students are encouraged to bring pictures from trips, labeled. Maps, globes, etc. are located at the center. The center could be structured with questions like: how far is this from our city; what modes of transportation might be used; give precise location with longitude, latitude; etc.

To avoid a traffic jam at favorite centers, most teachers structure who goes to which center. If students are in groups, groups can be assigned on a rotating basis to each center.

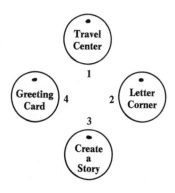

Secondary classroom can simply use row or table number to rotate groups.

Both choices and centers require more time and materials than previous examples of warmups and sponges. Yet, they offer a multi-modality approach to learning that is often lacking during instruction. They also offer a chance for students to move about the room productively!

SUMMARY

Effective sponges meet the following criteria:

-are short
-require little or no materials
-are easy enough for all students
-are FUN for the students

The benefits of using sponge activities are many:

-provide a short practice period on previously learned material
-increase time on task
-decrease the likelihood of management problems while students are "waiting"
-provide a mental set for a new lesson

TRANSITIONS: EFFECTIVE DIRECTION GIVING

Does this sound familiar: "Oh, no! They've done it just like I told them." Or, "I'm telling you for the last time."

Teachers are continually giving directions. With every change of activity, directions are usually required. At the elementary level, common transitions include: entering the classroom, finishing work, getting into reading groups, going to and from recess and lunch, going to "specials" (music, art, gym, etc.), switching subjects. At the secondary level, there is a typical pattern of activity during the period: opening, checking/grading papers, lecture/discussion, seatwork, then closing. If these are not established routines that happen automatically, then each shift requires a new set of directions. If the transition is unstructured, teachers can anticipate an increase in disruptive behaviors (Arlin, 1979). Because of this "guarantee", the best defense is a good offense — structure the transition.

In preparing for transitions, Arlin suggests the following:

1. bring momentum to a halt
2. announce change allowing students time to shift gears
3. time transition carefully — if most of class is intensely focused on previous activity, it may not be appropriate to shift activities at this time.

One elementary teacher was observed using a transition song. He began singing this particular song whenever students were to put work away and give him undivided attention. Students joined in singing as they cleaned up. By the last verse, all desks were clear. Students were ready for the new activity. The singing maintained focus of those who cleaned up early and discouraged them from initiating contacts with others.

In addition to preparing for the transition, teachers may need to give a new set of directions for the next activity. Before giving these directions, some quick mental planning should include:

1. How many steps are there to the directions? When more than two, put them in writing or pictographs.
2. If a natural order exists, sequence the directions. If

the directions are for a complicated worksheet, it might be best to distribute worksheets first, then give directions while students have model to refer to.

3. If directions include a combination of activities (like forming special groups, getting materials, and steps for working with materials) — accomplish one activity before giving directions for the next. For example, have students physically move into their new groups before having them get materials. After materials are distributed, give specific directions for using materials.

Steps in giving each set of directions look very much like those in teaching any lesson. But, instead of taking 20 or 30 minutes as in teaching a lesson, the steps take two or three minutes.

1. *Signal:* Why bother giving directions if some students aren't listening? You'll only have to repeat them again . . . and again . . . again. "I'm going to tell you one more time and this time you'd better listen!"

2. *Give the directions:* Keep them short and to the point. When we unnecessarily elaborate, we only add confusion. One teacher was heard giving these directions:

"You need to raise your hand for this activity. You can also take notes if you want to. But, you really don't have to. Be sure to listen to what other people have to say. Of course, we always need good listening habits, but this time it is particularly important. So, don't be sitting too close to others because you might get distracted. You may only ask one question of the speaker and that question must demand either a yes or no answer. Some of you may have done this before, but it won't hurt to do it again. Remember, though, the hardest part is to not ask the same question as someone else in the class. Do you have any questions?" One brave soul raised his hand and said, "Yeah, what are we supposed to do?"

It would make the task easier for students to simply list: 1. Raise your hand. 2. Ask questions requiring only a yes or no answer. 3. Don't repeat questions others have asked.

3. If possible, *give students a visual model of what is expected of them.* If they are to circle an adjective and underline a noun in each sentence, put an example of what this looks like on the board. If directions involve physical

"OK Class, get your books off your desk."

Effective teachers were clearer in giving directions.
Emmer & Evertson, 1980

movement, have one table or a few students demonstrate while others watch.

4. *Check students to be sure they understand* before turning them loose. Have everyone do the first problem together before asking, "Do you all understand?" Many times directions sound clear to students and it's not until they try to follow them that questions appear. Asking another student to paraphrase your directions not only lets you know if students understand, it gives students a chance to hear them given in "peer" terms. (if the directions are complicated, students may need guided practice on the first problem or step: "Let's all do the first one together. Look up here when you're done." (pause) "This is what your answer should look like. How many of you got that? Now, are there any questions?"

5. *GO!* If all students have materials in front of them, it's possible to begin at once. However, if movement is required to another place, a traffic jam can be avoided if controlled by the teacher. Calling on one table at a time, or just the boys, or by birthday months (or whatever!) smooths the way into the next activity.

CHAPTER 5
The Law of Least Intervention

*Techniques for Handling
Minor Disruptions in the Classroom*

It would be so easy if all we had to do was teach. In some classrooms this might be the case. Students are sitting in their seats, waiting eagerly for instruction. Discipline is not a problem—at least, not a major one. Credit for such a productive classroom is often given to the management strategies teachers use with students. In particular, teaching standards and routines at the beginning of the year encourages productive student behavior. Providing short practice activities or warm-ups at the beginning and end of classes eliminates potentially wasted time that could brew trouble. Providing interesting and relevant examples makes it easier to listen. Maintaining a rapid pace with a strong accountability system built in doesn't leave time for inattention.

The fact is, however, in spite of these proactive management strategies and efforts to present a good lesson, students will engage in minor disruptive activities: chatting while the teacher is talking, passing notes and roughhousing. It's not possible to eliminate this behavior completely with proactive management, but it is possible to minimize it. Instead of giving in to the belief that kids are worse than they used to be and that the usual techniques no longer work, effective teachers develop alternative strategies. For example, one teacher from a large urban district was overheard complaining that he trembled whenever he turned his back on his class for fear of what might happen. The teacher from the room next to him responded by saying that she'd learned that *avoiding* turn-

61

ing her back to the class was an excellent way of maintaining control. The difference between the reactive and
proactive attitudes was reflected in both the number and
severity of problems these two teachers experienced.

Effective managers are intuitively using the *Law of Least
Intervention* in handling minor misbehavior. They realize
that when this type of misbehavior is not eliminated immediately, there is a risk of a snowballing effect. Instead
of two students chatting, half the class is soon involved.
What began as minor roughhousing turns into aggressive
fighting. Kids learn by example what they can "get away
with." It is the "job" of adolescents, in particular, to test
the limits of the classroom. The teacher who is trying to
provide maximum time on task and reduce the severity
of management problems is faced with the problem of
eliminating this type of misbehavior without losing
valuable teaching time.

"Traditional" Strategies for Minor Misbehavior
The alternatives for handling such disruptions are many.
While most will temporarily stop the disruption, it is
necessary to consider the ultimate effect of the alternative.
The severe disciplinarian with the "don't smile 'til
Christmas" philosophy may administer punishment,
regardless of the degree or severity of misbehavior. While
immediate order is regained, the teacher risks both
unpleasant feeling tones as well as an "I'll get even with
you" threat—and kids don't have to play by the same rules
as teachers. (Ask any secondary teacher who's had their
name inscribed for posterity on a lavoratory wall.) There's
also the cumulative effect of continued unpleasant feelings in a classroom. A student's negative feelings at that
instant may spread to negative feelings toward both teacher
and subject matter, as well as a generalized negative feeling toward school.

Resorting to more aggressive techniques for dealing with
discipline problems presents the teacher as a negative role
model. Often, the teacher's response to the problem causes
greater disruption to the learning environment than did
the student's. For example, two students are chatting at

"We need to recognize that the way of responding to an individual child will have an effect on the rest of the class. The ways in which punishment is used and the frequency with which it is given will carry messages to **other** children, and create an atmosphere which can run counter to the intended effect on the offending individual."

Rutter, et.al., 1979

their seats while the teacher is working with a small group; the teacher shouts over the heads of the rest of the class (who are working quietly alone). A mini-sermonette is delivered and the entire class is both interrupted as well as uneasy. While the unpleasant message wasn't directed toward them specifically, they can't help but experience its effect.

In an effort to avoid being the tough disciplinarian and creating those unpleasant feeling tones, some teachers chose to ignore the behavior, hoping it will go away. This risk is too great. Once misbehavior escalates, the teacher will be forced to deal with it. This time the choice of alternatives is limited. The required forceful intervention is likely to produce even more unpleasant feeling tones as well as stronger retaliatory intentions.

In addition to ignoring or overreacting to minor misbehavior, some teachers fall into the trap of using the "nagging reminder". "How many times do I have to tell you not to comb your hair in class, Kevin?"
"This is the last time I'm going to tell you to get back in your seat, Mike."

Again, this strategy serves only to temporarily stop the problem. As it continues to repeat itself, the teacher usually has to resort to a more aggressive strategy. One teacher was observed making the following comments over a five minute period of time: "I can't hear, you're too noisy." "Sh, sh. . . . excuse me!" "I'm getting tired of having to shout." Finally, in desperation, he told the class they would all have to make up ten minutes after school for not working quietly. Feelings of the students toward the class and teacher were far from positive that day.

Rationale
The Law of Least Intervention fills the gap between just plain ignoring and forceful intervention. It organizes alternatives on a continuuum from those taking the least amount of teacher time as well as least amount of interruption of the learning environment to those that require

both time and some interruption of teaching activity. The goals of this continuum of choices are:

1. to maintain a positive feeling tone in the classroom — a characteristic of effective schools
2. to maximize time on task—more time devoted to learning
3. to present a positive role model
4. to avoid generalized negative feelings toward teacher, school, and subject

These goals are accomplished by handling minor misbehavior in a way that: takes the LEAST amount of time, LEAST amount of teacher effort, LEAST unpleasant feelings, and creates the LEAST disruption to the learning environment.

Automatic Scanner

The one requirement to using the *"Law"* is that the teacher must have an automatic scanner going at all times. That is, the teacher must continually scan all students in the classroom. This will not only prevent some misbehavior from occurring, it will also spot misbehavior immediately, before it has a chance to escalate. Think of the automobile driver about to run a yellow light. The driver quickly and automatically looks around for any sign of law enforcement officers. If spotted, the decision is made to stop for the light. If all is clear, the light is run. So it is in the classroom. Before Pedro shares gum with some classmates, he glances in the direction of the teacher. Should the ever-moving eyes of the teacher meet Pedro's, gum sharing is likely to be done later. If not, gum may be shared. Pedro's neighbors may try to get his attention to get some. Soon the number of students off task has increased to the point that the teacher is forced to intervene.

Effective managers are described as "having eyes in the back of their head". This is the teacher who is able to carry on a conversation with another person in the front of the room while the scanner continues to move. When these teachers are working with small groups, the groups are situated in the front of the room. Students have their backs to the rest of the class so the teacher can face the entire room, with scanner going. While the automatic scanner may stop a potential misbehavior, it also communicates high expectations: expectations that students should be on task. High expectations are characteristic of effective teachers and effective schools.

Should the automatic scanner spot minor misbehavior, teacher decision making is put into gear. The decision is whether to react to the problem or ignore it. As already mentioned, there is a risk that ignoring misbehavior may cause escalation of the problem Yet, there is some off-task behavior that can safely be ignored.

Kids are off task briefly and return to attention before teacher intervenes. When this happens, it would be the teacher who creates the disturbance in the classroom by reacting to the incident. If the teacher feels compelled to let these students know they were "spotted", then dealing with them at another time, individually, might be best.

Sometimes it is clear that whatever the offense, it will neither spread nor disrupt others. For example, if a student fails to put materials away properly, this can be dealt with at a later time.

USING THE LAW OF LEAST INTERVENTION
If the teacher decision is to stop a disruption immediately, with the least interruption, possible strategies might include:

> eye contact
> physical closeness
> pause
> "the look"
> touch/gesture
> asking for response
> praising desirable behavior
> Grandma's Law
> cueing
> humor

Eye Contact

Now it is time for the automatic scanner to stop. The teacher makes direct and prolonged eye contact with the student who has just poked a neighbor or whispered to a friend. The non-verbal message is "I saw what happened. Don't let it happen again." The rest of the class is not even aware of strategy as the teacher continues to teach, not changing tone of voice or expression. Should the teacher decide this strategy will not be effective (i.e. the student will not look the teacher in the eye or several students are involved), it's necessary to move down the continuum of alternatives.

Physical Closeness

The teacher who is able to continue explaining or asking questions while moving about the room can stop problems with physical presence. To be the "teacher on roller skates" necessitates having desks or tables arranged to allow immediate access to all students. Tethering oneself to the overhead projector, chalkboard, or stool encourages open season on off-task behavior from students in the corners of the classroom. Getting physically close to off-task students also allows for the direct eye contact that may not have been possible earlier as "guilty" students may be reluctant to look at the teacher.

This strategy is particularly effective during group discussion. When another student is speaking it is often difficult for students in opposite corners of the classroom to hear. To fill the void, they may "create" their own activity. The teacher could walk in their direction. This physical closeness will both cause immediate focus as well as encourage the student answering to speak up so everyone can hear.

Pause

The continual drone of the teacher's voice sometimes provides the "cover" some students need to engage in other than productive behaviors. Whispering to neighbors is not likely to be noticed if the teacher's voice masks additional noises! When the automatic scanner spots this unwanted activity, a prolonged pause in instruction may encourage

"The Look"

Effective managers would move near to the inattentive students, use eye contact where possible . . . "

Brophy, 1982

immediate silence from all. If there are many students off task, this strategy is not as effective.

"The Look"
Every teacher has one! It takes only an instant to deliver and is best given when the rest of the class is engaged in independent seatwork or small group work. In addition to the direct eye contact, it conveys the message "I mean it!" Combining the look with body posture leaning toward the student and having one hand on the student's desk causes some students to "melt"!

Touch/Gesture
A hand on a student's shoulder can be a reminder to change inappropriate behavior. It may add to the sincerity of the eye contact and may communicate much more than words. Remembering that need to retain positive feelings, the touch is a gentle one—not the finger squeeze to the back of the neck that many of us may have experienced in our school days! For the "out of seat" student, simply pointing to his desk may be a more positive reminder of appropriate behavior than the wagging finger and accompanying frown. Simply shaking your head when a student puts her feet on a neighbor's desk will be a more pleasant reminder than interrupting the class to tell her where her feet belong.

Asking for Response
It's possible to tune out conversation completely—until you hear your name spoken. While walking recently at the airport, engaged in thought and oblivious to the continual announcements on the loud speaker, I was brought back to "reality" on hearing "Cummings". Not having heard the message given before the name, I had to listen for the announcer to repeat it. This happens in classrooms daily—but many times the consequences are unpleasant. The student is absorbed in conversation with another. The teacher, in an attempt to bring her back on task, says "What were the types of rock I just listed, Mia?" On hearing her name, Mia looks up. Yet, not having listened to the teacher's explanation earlier (let alone the question), she doesn't know the answer. This can lead to embarrassment and insecurity. Some students may deal with this

threat to social security with an attention-getting or hostile response. This tends to escalate a relatively minor situation and forces a more aggressive teacher response.

Good and Brophy (1978) suggest a more effective use of the name strategy: call name first and ask a question that the student can answer successfully. "Mia (pause), did you study types of rock in your science class last year?" Now, Mia heard the question because her name alerted her and the question wasn't dependent upon her having listened to what the teacher had been saying earlier.

Praising Desirable Behavior
Many of the strategies mentioned so far will be most effective when dealing with only one or two students. When the numbers increase, addressing the group as a whole may be necessary. Yet, it does not need to be negative. Finding some students who are displaying appropriate behavior is all that's needed. "This table has done a great job on getting started on their assignment. They're half finished."—a gentle reminder to be on task. "Thank you for raising your hand and waiting to be called upon, Chico." This may even work on the student guilty of the misbehavior. Chico may have blurted out a previous response and the teacher chose to ignore it the first time. The teacher consciously tried to "catch the child being good".

Praising desirable behavior can backfire with older students if used inappropriately. Singling a student out for good behavior can cause others to tease or make fun of the student. It's best to give the praise for appropriate behavior annonymously or privately.

Grandma's Law
Grandmas have been considered clever in how they've managed to have grandchildren finish their meals: "As soon as you finish your potatoes, you may have a piece of your favorite chocolate cake!" This same strategy works well when the class is getting noisy: "If you can work quietly on your assignment for the next ten minutes, we'll have time for a game of seven-up." When the teacher makes

an activity that students' enjoy (i.e. game) contingent upon appropriate behavior (i.e.working quietly), Grandma's Law is being used. This is likely to be much more effective than sounding like the broken record "Class, I'm getting tired of reminding you to quiet down."

Cueing
Finding a response that is not compatible with the undesired behavior can often stop the disruption without even mentioning it! "Class, take out scratch paper and list three words that will be found between these guide words. I'll walk around to check your answers." Having to get out paper may stop the note passing in the back row, talking over in the corner of the room, and Larry's folding a paper airplane. Asking a question that requires everyone to respond physically or verbally can stop annoying disruptions like a student tapping a pencil on a desk or working on an assignment for another class. "I'll give you a word; you raise one arm if there is only one syllable, two arms if you hear two." "Let's all stand and touch our toes ten times." Or, "Put your heads down on your desks and try to visualize what's happening as I describe the next battle." The class is back on task without ever stopping the lesson.

Humor
When all else fails, we might have to stop instruction to remind the class of appropriate behavior. Keeping a sense of humor in light of the situation, though, may be better than sounding like the powerful authority figure. To an unusually noisy class, a second grade teacher cupped her hands over her mouth and said "Space shuttle to earth, can you hear me!" Students turned around in their seats, grinning, and were back on task.

SUMMARY
The ideas in the *Law of Least Intervention* aren't new— but it's the conscious and consistent use of them that makes the difference between a positive or negative classroom climate. The effective manager will also recognize the difference between the minor misbehavior and the more severe case. Eye contact won't stop an ag-

gressive fight between students. And, Grandma's Law is worthless when there's threat of physical or property damage. But, if it's any consolation, the teacher using the *Law of Least Intervention* at the right time and place will have fewer instances of severe disruptions in the classroom. The classroom becomes a pleasant place for both students and teacher.

Quality Time On Task

The remaining chapters will focus on *how* time is spent in the classroom. We have enough evidence now to conclude that all time on task is not qualitatively the same. Specific instructional strategies promote basic skills achievement.Holding all students accountable for questions promotes greater learning . Recent brain research demonstrates that we need to expand traditional instructional strategies to even begin to tap our potential. Social psychologists have demonstrated the positive effects of learning in cooperative groups—a change in how we organize our time.Spending more time in affective education may make both management of the classroom easier as well as motivate students in the subject. And, we have a clearer understanding now how to motivate minority students.

Finding more time for learning — more time on task — will benefit us only if we spend that extra time wisely. Otherwise, we may reverse our efforts to create a productive learning environment. If students are not successful, dislike the subject or teacher's style, they may in turn become bored . . . behavior problems. The teacher is put in the position of having to react . . . and a vicious cycle has begun.

The following chapters will explore ideas on *quality* time on task.

CHAPTER 6
Learning In Cooperative Groups

Cooperative grouping is a way of organizing the classroom for learning. Students work together in small groups to complete worksheets, study for tests, and solve problems. The benefits of this structure accrue in the areas of classroom management for the teacher as well as cognitive and affective growth for the student.

The ability to work with others is almost a prerequisite to success in this world. Students must cooperate in sports (i.e. basketball team), in clubs (i.e. scouts), in their family, as well as any work related activitiy. One goal of public education is to prepare youth to be contributing members of society. Cooperative learning groups provide that important time on task to develop the skill.

Yet, cooperative grouping rarely occurs. Traditional classrooms are generally competitive. A competitive environment develops competitive individuals—one student's success is another's failure. American students will give up rewards for themselves in order to have their opponents lose — more so than Mexican-American or black students. In contrast, opportunity to work in small groups increases group cohesiveness and mutual concern among classmates (Slavin, 1980).

Cooperative grouping fosters academic achievement. Mastery learning advocates have demonstrated that given enough time and appropriate instruction, virtually all children can learn (Bloom, 1976). Yet, teachers hestitate to continue teaching when most of the group "has it". To avoid boring those students who have grasped the lesson, the class is given the assignment for independent seatwork while the teacher runs around trying to answer questions

Cartoon by Jerry Melton
Birmingham School
District, Michigan

Less effective managers often give students too much information at once.

Anderson, Evertson & Emmer, 1980

from the students who need more TIME. While waiting for help, arm waving in the air, students often find other diversions—distracting students trying to work. Cooperative learning groups provide the means by which students can have their questions answered immediately by their peers—more time to learn and practice, less time waiting.

Students need opportunity to practice new material, but it is generally accomplished alone. Yet, research supports group instruction—not totally independent — as most effective for learning. Students are more engaged during groupwork (Rosenshine, 1980). One only has to walk into a classroom and observe students after they have been working alone a period of time. They get restless...looking for excuses to go to the bathroom or pencil sharpener...or to whisper to a friend. Chances are, they are looking for social contacts!

One middle school educator (A. Arth, University of Wyoming) suggests that group work be an integral part of the class period. He suggests that teachers plan lessons around the quarter system:

1/4 teacher talk
1/4 large group discussion; student questions
1/4 small group work
1/4 independent-alone time

Using this formula, a lesson might begin with students doing a warm-up activity for ten minutes (alone at desk). The teacher then introduces the new lesson for another ten minutes. The next ten minutes are spent discussing and answering questions about the new lesson. During the last ten minutes, small groups form to work cooperatively on a worksheet together. The formula eliminates extensive periods of working alone or extensive teacher talk.

Increases in student achievement has been a consistent outcome in the cooperative learning research (Slavin, 1980). Students may become discipline problems when they view the classroom as a negative environment, one in which they have little chance to succeed. Low achievers may feel that no matter how hard they try, they'll never be at the same level as high achievers. Unless the pattern is stopped, this belief may become a self-fulfilling prophecy for them.

Cooperative talk in small groups may also be a preferred style of learning for many students (Dunn & Dunn, 1978). Thus, in addition to extra time for learning, they provide the appropriate style of instruction for many students. The design of the traditional classroom—a competitive atmosphere—may create too high a level of concern for minority students. (See chapter: Motivation and Minority Students)

WHY WE DON'T USE GROUPS

Recognizing the advantages of cooperative learning groups, why don't we see more of them in classrooms? Most teachers have tried them for art, social studies, and science projects. A frequent reaction to them is that they create discipline problems rather than eliminate them. It's easier for the teacher to maintain control with 30 students working alone in silence. When groups are together, noise level escalates and peers influence one another to get off task. Teachers are faced with comments like "I don't want to work with him." or "Don't put me next to her!" Time is lost in handling these complaints. Problems escalate because a disliked student may cover up by becoming even more of a bully. Frustrated, teachers either give the class the admonition that they need to learn to work together; or, they rearrange the environment (back to working alone) to avoid the hassle.

Generally, groups have been informal, often formed by students getting to choose who they want to work with. The end result may be groups of all high or all low achievers; or, groups formed because of ethnic group or color. Feelings are hurt when students are the last to be selected by peers or there is open hostility. Racial tension is increased rather than lessened. These experiences seem to contradict what researchers are saying—that groups encourage mutual concern for others, increase self esteem, and increase positive race relations. Why?

78

There is a "science" to establishing and maintaining cooperative learning groups that didn't exist when most teachers received their professional training. First, students can't be mandated that they work cooperatively any more than they can be mandated to master math or spelling. Consistent with the theme of this book, students need to be taught—not told—behavioral expectations, routines, and work requirements. The procedures and social skills necessary for effective group work also need to be taught. An accountability system that is characteristic of the proactive classroom manager is equally important for group-work as it is for individual work. A task analysis of cooperative groups should include:

PROCEDURAL
- selecting team members
- how to get into and out of groups
- signal to gain attention while in groups
- how to seek help
- behavioral expectations (i.e. voice level)
- what to do if finish early
- accountability system (i.e. grading, rewards)
- what to do with completed papers

SOCIAL SKILLS
- friendship
- discussion/communication
- leadership
- conflict resolution

TYPE OF GROUP
- informal
- formal

PROCEDURAL

Most team learning models have teachers choosing team members. This can be done randomly—counting off in class, drawing names from hat—or in a structured manner. Random group assignment may not provide a good group balance to encourage tutoring, however. Teams may comprise all high or all low achievers. The Johns Hopkins model (Slavin, 1980) recommends balancing teams by ability, race, and sex. A team of four might consist of one high achiever, two average, and one low achiever. If the

"Children are very quick to pick up other people's expectations about both their academic competence and their behavior . . . people tend to live up (or down) to what is expected of them."

Rutter et.al., 1979

class has equal numbers of boys and girls and a racial balance of three quarters majority and one quarter minority, each team would reflect this balance. Teacher choice of team composition eliminates likes choosing likes and more evenly distributes ability levels in groups. It also helps break the often rigid friendship patterns where students stay together because they are from the same neighborhood, previous class, church or club.

Getting into groups signals another transition time—a time when discipline problems double. Anticipating the potential problems, a routine needs to be established such that minimal disruption occurs. It makes it easier when students already sit around the same table or their desks are close and have only to be turned slightly to face one another. If teams are meeting in various locations around the room, a chart or transparency showing each group's location eliminates confusion and traffic jams. It's not unusual to hear "I've forgotten which group I'm in. Where do I go?" when names are simply read from a list.

How do groups get worksheets or materials needed? Having one student assigned the responsibility of being team monitor to get team materials may eliminate wait time. Should a group finish early, what are their alternatives or choices of activities? Letting students know how much time they will have in groups allows them to pace themselves. A kitchen timer, set for the designated time provides a visual reminder.

What are the behavioral expectations during group work? Appropriate voice level should be taught (i.e. use inside not outside voice) as well as what the teacher's cue will be if voices exceed limit. Three blinks of the light switch or just turning off lights may be a better cue than the nagging reminder "Class, you are too noisy."

How does group work influence a student's grade? Some classes grade on cooperation and participation within the group. Teachers walk around and tally such behavior! Others take the group score on the worksheet or average individual quizzes to get a group score. There are drawbacks to having group scores determine grades. A high achiever's efforts may be fruitless if other team members fail to perform. A compromise grading system might have individual quiz scores contribute directly to grade while group averages contribute to various forms of team recognition and reward. (The Johns Hopkins model for team learning has developed an elaborate system of improvement points to reconcile the grading issue.)

What other incentives (besides grades) encourage group work? The reward system may be anywhere from simply posting team scores weekly with verbal encouragement to tangible rewards such as stickers and prizes. A middle school teacher took a Polaroid picture of the winning team each week and posted it beside the chart of team scores. Monthly or weekly newsletters might be written highlighting winning teams. Below is a sample newsletter from one class just beginning team work:

THE MATH REPORTER
KIDS WIZ CLASS

The Wiz Kids (Andrew, Jason, Mikel, and Shin) whizzed their way into first place on the first week on team math. The BDSS Bombers nosed in for second (Bill, Dom, Sadie and Sabrina) on the fine performance by Dom and Sabrina getting 10 points each.

THIS WEEK'S RANK		SCORE
1st	Wiz Kids	39
2nd	Bombers	36
3rd	Androgenarians	34
4th	No Names	31
5th	Rubber Ducks	30
6th	Stars	29
7th	Masterminds	26

The next quiz will include measurement, perimeter and area of a rectangle.

Good luck!

Mrs. Click

---

*Written by Peggy Click, Vancouver, Washington

SOCIAL SKILLS
FRIENDSHIP

When was the last time someone told you to stop worrying and you did? Likewise, when was the last time you told students (or your own children) they needed to get along with one another and they did? Social skills need to be taught. Activities are needed to promote friendship and strengthen bonds of attraction. It is particularly important to provide these activities when a team is initially formed — before they attempt working with cognitive-type assignments. If the student doesn't feel liked in the group, he likely will not use his potential to the fullest. This isn't just the actively disliked child or the class scapegoat; the isolate or loner needs to feel that he has something to contribute to the group. Activities to promote friendship within the group include:

1. Completing a team profile by filling in a list of sentence starters:

> "We are a team that is very good at . . . "
> really like . . .
> dislike . . .
> wish that . . .

Teams might design a book cover or make a poster to illustrate the profile. Younger students might cut magazine pictures to create a picture collage. Selecting a team name based on the profile each team develops creates a team identity. Henceforth, teams can be referred to by name: the Munch Bunch, Dependables, Question Marks, etc.

*Many of these ideas are adapted from Project SELF: Orcutt Union School District, Orcutt, CA.

2. Teammate Bingo: How many Bingos can each team get? Quiz team members to find a person who (has):

same size shoe	traveled out of U.S.	had braces	likes to read
jogs 3 times a week	same number of brothers	reads the comics	likes same sports
broken a bone	likes same TV show	never moved	likes school
same kind of pet	same birthday month	likes spinach	had the measles

The same type of activity can be designed as WHO'S WHO: In our group, the person who —

is tallest is _____
is youngest is _____
has the most brothers and sisters is _____
is absent least is _____
watches the least television is _____
plays the most sports is _____

3. Adjective Hunt: The class is given a long list of positive adjectives (i.e., joking, nice, musical, great, gentle). Team members are asked to select three adjectives to describe each member. Silhouettes or portraits of each member might be made for a bulletin board display, with adjectives listed.

COMMUNICATION/DISCUSSION/LEADERSHIP

There seems to be one person in every group willing to do the work—talk the most, give the answers, etc. There might also be a clown or joker, continually taking the group off task. Or there may be students who just don't bother listening or contributing. Activities can be structured to make students aware of these problems:

1. Fair share: A recorder can be appointed to tally how many times each team member contributes or participates in the group. The group can be given a simple task—such as select a team slogan or motto (one that everyone agrees on). The recorder tallies group responses.

2. Chart a listener: After teaching the class attributes of a good listener, a recorder can tally when team members are demonstrating those characteristics. The group can be given a simple task—pick one person (movie star, politician, etc.) you all admire. While the other members of the group complete the task, the recorder is busy observing and tallying listening skills. Teams or the large group debrief afterwards by discussing what students were good at or what needs to be improved.

	Sandy	Al	Maggie	Karen
looks at speaker	II	I	I	
nods, to show "listening"	III	II		II
asks ?s to have speaker give details			I	I

3. Chart teamwork: Teach (define, give examples, etc.) how team members can encourage, contribute ideas, keep things cool, organize ideas, keep things on track, and ask questions. Have groups practice these skills. Again, the groups can be given a simple task, while a recorder tallies. Teamwork characteristics may be introduced two at a time per lesson, gradually building up to charting all at once. For example, only chart the skills "encourages" and "contributes ideas" during the first practice session. Recorders could also be rotated each lesson.

	Brian	Dot	Mina	Rufus
encourages				
contributes ideas				
keeps things cool				
organizes ideas				
keeps things on track				
asks questions				

An alternative to the charting idea might be to distribute cards to each team member (i.e. 3 cards saying "organize"; 3 cards saying "contribution"; 2 saying "encouragement"; 1 saying "keeping on track"). To make a contribution in the group, a person must play the card labeling the kind of contribution he is making. While this slows the discussion down, the need to label really causes members to think about the statements they make.

TYPES OF GROUPS
INFORMAL
Groups may meet randomly or on a routine basis, such as daily or every other day. At the elementary level they may work together for only one subject area or many. Many teachers find that math is an easy subject area to begin cooperative groups. The length of time to keep the same students in a group is also arbitrary. Keeping the same teams together for a period of time (4 to 6 weeks) is important if new friendships are to develop. Yet, it is just as important to change group composition after a period of time to prevent management problems and encourage multiple friendships.

Within the group students may work on only one worksheet and turn it in as a group product; or, work on individual worksheets checking with others if help is needed. Another way to use groups is to have students do a homework assignment independently, then meet in groups the next day to submit one paper to turn in to represent the group. This, again, works well in math as students can check answers with one another and rework questionable problems.

FORMAL
JIGSAW
Jigsaw (Aronson, 1978) is a form of groupwork where students are forced to rely on one another as resources. It works particulary well in social studies and literature assignments. The teacher identifies a general topic, then breaks it down into the same number of subtopics as there are students in a group. Each student must learn (read) about his particular subtopic, meet with members from other teams studying same topic to discuss and become expert in that subtopic, then meet with own group to teach that information to the rest of the team. Students soon learn that each member has a unique contribution to make. It is imperative to practice good listening skills because students will take individual quizzes at the end of the unit that cover the material taught by teammates.

A typical jigsaw lesson might proceed as follows: The subject, World War II, has been divided into the topics of German involvement, English involvement, Japanese involvement, and United States involvement. The teacher provides a mental set introducing the unit. Students read the section from their text discussing their particular sub-topic. Expert groups meet to discuss what they have read. If a student's topic was U.S. involvement in WW II, he will meet with that expert group to rehearse what he needs to teach his teammates. The teacher acts as a facilitator, monitoring the various groups. Students return to their jigsaw groups and teach one another their unique piece of the puzzle. Quizzes given at the end of the unit are taken individually and contain questions from all topics.

TEAMS-GAMES-TOURNAMENTS (TGT)

TGT grouping is a highly motivating team structure for learning basic skills (Slavin, 1980). The format includes: teacher presentation of material; teams study worksheets together during the week; then individuals compete in tournaments to bring points back to their own team. Tournament tables comprise three students of similar academic ability. By keeping ability levels the same at the tables, every student has an equal chance of bringing points back to their own team.

STUDENT TEAMS-
ACHIEVEMENT DIVISION (STAD)

STAD is particularly effective in basic skills learning (Slavin, 1980). It is a simpler structure than jigsaw, not quite as exciting for students as TGT — but it is quieter! The format includes teacher presentation of material and teams studying worksheets together during the week. However, it differs from TGT in that individual quizzes are given instead of a tournament. Students contribute points to their team score based on their improvement from previous quizzes. (Refer to the Johns Hopkins training manual for Student Team Learning for details on the elaborate scoring system.)

SUMMARY

The advantages to cooperative learning methods are many and varied. The focus of this book is to find more time during the classroom day for learning to occur. Groups can provide both quantity and quality time. As students learn to cooperate with one another, classroom problems decrease. Less time is spent with discipline. Certain minority and low-income groups who are more cooperative in their social orientation profit both academically and socially (Kagan, 1979).

CHAPTER 7
Attitudes

Student attitudes can interfere with maintaining a positive, productive classroom environment. There's the student who dislikes the subject being studied..."This stuff is boring." Or, the student who can't keep his hands off other's property. Or, the student who disagrees with any other point of view but his own. Or, the student who just doesn't share or take turns. Students with a low self concept as a learner are apt to be those who misbehave in the classroom (Purkey, 1978). What does one do with such students? Teachers can simply accept these attitudes and chalk the year off to a "bad one". Or, instructional time can be spent teaching in the affective domain. Affective education is the teaching of attitudes, values, and feelings.

Many district report cards grade students on affective objectives: works well with others, shows respect for authority, shows good sportsmanship, shows consideration for others. The question is, however, did teachers spend time teaching them? The research finding that more time on task is related to greater achievement is applicable in the affective as well as cognitive domain. Yet, a glance at most teacher plan books shows that most time on task is in cognitive areas. One study (Gansneder, Caldwell, Morris, Napier, & Bowen, 1977) found that only 14% of the major objectives of elementary teachers were in the affective domain and even these were at the lowest levels.

There are many reasons for neglecting the affective. There is a widespread belief that attitudes are "caught not taught". There's also the realization that an attitude can't be taught in a 30 minute lesson as math or other content can. The present demand for accountability and measurement of pupil growth almost forces teachers to teach to easily measurable objectives. Teaching affective lessons is like "planting seeds that grow over time" — time that outcome-based education may not provide.

Yet, we can't afford to ignore student attitudes that interfere with a productive environment. This chapter will explore ways to promote students attitudes such as

> respect for the property of others
> recognition of more than one acceptable point of view
> listening to others with respect
> observation of safety rules
> respect for concept of sharing
> positive self concept

The taxonomy of the affective domain (Krathwohl, Bloom, & Masia, 1964) provides a continuum of levels to describe affective behavior. With the taxonomy as the model, I will explore affective development through direct instruction, cognitive lessons, success, and modeling.

TAXONOMY OF THE AFFECTIVE DOMAIN

The major categories of affective behavior include receiving, responding, valuing, organizing, and characterization.

Receiving

The learner becomes aware of (passively attends to) information. The teacher is concerned with getting, holding, and directing student attention with a discussion, filmstrip, guest speaker, etc.

Responding

An activity is structured to encourage a "learning by doing" experience. The learner goes beyond just listening passively; instead, becomes involved in the subject and gains a sense of satisfaction from the participation. Willingly doing an assignment or obeying school rules are examples. The emphasis is on the student cooperating willingly, not out of fear of punishment.

Valuing

The student finds worth or value to a particular behavior or object. In a variety of situations, the student responds with a consistent "attitude". The behavior is now internalized—not a result complying with another's wishes.

Organization
An attitude or value may be relevant in one situation but may conflict with another value in a new situation. This level recognizes the need to build a value system whereby these conflicts are resolved. The student can identify how a new value relates to others he already holds.

Characterization
The student's value system has become so internalized and controlled his behavior for a long enough period of time that it describes his "life style." Educational objectives are not generally set at this level (Krathwohl et. al., 1964).

Typical Educational Objectives
Receiving
Awareness that there may be more than one acceptable point of view
Sensitivity to others' feelings
Awareness of good listening habits
Awareness of cultural differences

Responding
Willingness to cooperate in student team learning
Obeys classroom rules
Finishes assigned work
Practices safety rules on playground
Voluntarily participates in class discussion
Enjoys working with students of various ethnic backgrounds
Takes pleasure in helping others

Valuing
Desires to be a good citizen in class
Assumes responsibility for promoting cooperative teamwork
Appreciates the need for a classroom management system

Organization
Judges various ethnic groups on the basis of their behaviors as individuals
Makes decisions regarding the type of life he wants to lead

DIRECT INSTRUCTION

Direct instruction is applicable in the affective at the receiving and responding levels. Anything beyond these two levels is highly individualized—determined by the degree of internalization of the attitude in each student. Unfortunately, teaching attitudes through direct instruction typically stops at the receiving level. "Exhortation is used more and accomplished less than almost any behavior changing tool known to man" (Mager,1968). For example:

"Some of you are scribbling on desks—let's shape up and learn to respect property."

"The lunchroom is too noisy. Be considerate of others and let them eat at quiet tables."

Students become aware of the problem, attend to the "teacher admonition", and a few may have a chance to respond to teacher led discussion. At best, we might surmise that those FEW students involved in discussion were at the responding level.

Many students enter a lesson with preexisting attitudes. The opportunity to be exposed to their friends' feelings on a subject and to examine all sides of an issue may or may not change those feelings. Yet, it is only through their active participation and social interaction—not from our directives—that they change their belief system. This will take more time on task than we presently allow. It will also take more variety in teacher instructional strategies. The popular teacher-led, large-group discussion involves but a few students. If our affective goal is that the student feel that a behavior is important to him personally (valuing level), our lessons need to include ample opportunity for ALL students to participate at the responding level:

☆ *students voluntarily take their own position on an issue*

☆ *students experience satisfaction in doing so*

Thus, our lesson plans should include activities structured for both the receiving and responding levels. The activities selected at the responding level must be sufficiently motivating to the students to encourage the sense of satisfaction and the likelihood the student will value what is being taught. Encouraging students to respond with their own feelings can be hard for the teacher—who may not like what he hears! The teacher must assume the role of the "guide on the side", not the "sage on the stage." Below are three sample lesson plans:

OBJECTIVE: The learner will take turns in using equipment.
Receiving
　Discuss/list when it is necessary to take turns
　Attend to a film strip on sharing equipment
Responding
　In small groups, brainstorm consequences of not sharing equipment. Share personal feelings when having to work with others who don't share. List alternative ways of getting a turn.

OBJECTIVE: The learner will develop a positive self concept.
Receiving/Responding
　Student cuts out pictures from magazines describing himself; makes a collage
　Student lists people who think he's special
　Student brainstorms list of things he does well
　Student describes in writing what he'd like to do better; how he'll go about it
　Student completes a sentence starter(on the chalkboard) each day in journal: I feel good when I . . . Sometimes I feel like . . . Two things I like about myself are . . .

OBJECTIVE: The learner will consider multiple solutions and implications of solutions in handling problems.

Receiving

Discuss the things that happen at school that create anger and potential fights (i.e., cutting in line, shoving, name calling).

Each student lists the incidents that bother them most and how they typically handle the problem.

Volunteers role play various problem situations, demonstrating various solutions.

Responding

Fish bowl: A small group is formed within the larger group. A problem is identified and students in inner group offer potential solutions to that problem. "Someone got ink on your new shirt. What would you do?"

Small groups: Students discuss the implications or consequences of each solution offered during the fish bowl. They rank order the solutions from most effective to least.

This procedure of describing a problem, offering solutions via fish bowl, and small group discussion might be repeated several times each week (changing the problem each time).

Below are several strategies that are effective in motivating students to respond to an issue:

Small group discussion: The teacher can structure by providing discussion questions. How would you feel if it happened to you? What if everybody had the same view? Are there other alternatives you might accept?

Rank ordering: Students choose alternatives and arrange in order of their own preference—including a sentence or two explaining their choices.

Sentence completion: Sentence starters are provided. A problem or issue is discussed and students complete own sentences in light of the issue. My feeling is that . . . Most people would . . . I wouldn't . . . My wish is that . . .

Brainstorming: Students are taught the rules of brainstorming, then follow the procedure in small groups. A recorder is selected to write all suggestions. Common rules include: write down all suggestions; no put downs on anyone's ideas; it's O.K. to have far out suggestions; get quantity not quality; use other ideas to stimulate your own thinking.

Role playing: Students assume a new identity in a practice situation. They try to feel, think, and act like the new person. This is sometimes more productive if done in small groups to lessen the anxiety of having to "act" in front of the class.

DURING COGNITIVE LESSONS

We've all had students who "just don't like math" or some particular subject. Many times it is these same students who don't like the subject that become our management problems. Including affective questions with a cognitive lesson may give students opportunity to become aware of and respond in a positive way toward the subject. Below are examples of such questions:

-List ways that the skill of reading will help you as an adult.
-Choose an explorer you particularly like; share your feelings why.
-When does math help you at home?
-If you had been the President that year, would you have made the same decisions?
-Make up sentences about yourself that use some of your spelling words.
-Which chapter from our text did you enjoy the most? Why?
-What kinds of books can you read the longest without losing interest?
-Today I realized that . . . I learned that . . . I was pleased that . . . I was displeased that . . .

Students might respond to such questions in a journal at the beginning or end of class; they might answer on a slip of paper and use it as a "ticket out the door"; or, such questions might be used as small group discussion topics.

WE LIKE
YOUR
ATTITUDE

Student

Teacher

Principal

(Developed by Edmonds School District, Lynnwood, WA)

SUPER PERSON

SUCCESS/PAYOFF

Which subjects were your favorite in school? What sport do you enjoy? Chances are that whatever your favorites, you have been successful in them. It's not likely that we would enjoy a subject that we do poorly in. Likewise, in constructing activities at the responding level. it is important that students experience a positive emotional reaction by participating. If students experience fear, anxiety, frustration, embarrassment, or boredom, they are less likely to develop the value or appreciation we are teaching.

One teacher was observed doing choral reading of a poem with her class. Students were enjoying the experience — until the culminating activity. They were given a quiz on the content of the poem. That look of pleasure on the faces of the youngsters turned into one of frustration in trying to answer the cognitive questions. The affective objective, to develop appreciation of poetry, was not accomplished. Likewise, when students experience frustration and lack of success in cognitive activities, the cognitive learning may have taken place at the expense of liking the content.

Structure the environment to provide positive consequences for learners when they demonstrate an attitude we are trying to influence. Certificates signed by the principal and teacher can recognize attitudes we are trying to foster:

We Like Your Attitude
Humanitarian Award
You've Been Coming Prepared
Award For Outstanding Effort In A Group
Is Hooked On Books
Outstanding Effort

Specific praise encourages students to exhibit that same behavior in the future. "You are really working quietly. It is easier for all of us to learn when you help make school a pleasant place to be." "The way you encouraged your teammates to take turns made your team successful. Thank you."

Reactive management strikes again!

" . . . pupils are likely to be influenced . . . either for good or ill by the models of behavior provided by teachers . . . "

Rutter et.al., 1979

Effective managers would not "interrupt the lesson unnecessarily by delivering extended reprimands or other overreactions. That would focus everyone's attention on the inattentive students rather than the lesson content."

Brophy, 1982

MODELING

Many of our behaviors weren't learned from direct experience, but rather from observing other people's behaviors. One classic experiment demonstrated that children behaved the same way toward a doll as they had observed an adult model acting. Those students observing aggressive behavior, demonstrated aggressive behavior; likewise, non-aggressive modeling produced non-aggressive children. There are many implications from this research for teachers. The behaviors we hope to see in students, we encourage by modeling ourselves:

> politeness
> respect for students
> commitment to learning
> respect for good thinking
> enthusiasm for subject matter

The list goes on! The list could also reflect negative behaviors modeled:

> messy desk
> late to class
> sarcasm
> sloppy appearance
> disliking subject matter

(One teacher was overheard commenting, "I don't like studying grammar any more than you do . . . but it's a requirement!")

Obviously, learning by imitation is unlimited in both its negative and positive consequences.

SUMMARY

Teachers can't INSIST that students have positive attitudes . . . but they can ASSIST. Providing more time in affective activities, building the affective into cognitive lessons, and modeling the behaviors we hope to promote can only pay off in better management and more learning.

CHAPTER 8
Accountability Through Questioning

Can you remember having a teacher you wouldn't dream of being a problem for? Not because that teacher was an autocratic ruler, but because you just didn't have time time to even think of other things to do? That teacher kept you so involved in the lesson there wasn't time to chat with a neighbor or pass a note. Chances are, that teacher excelled in what researchers call "momentum" and accountability (Kounin, 1970). In fact, it seems as if one of the hallmarks of successful class management is keeping pupils actively engaged in productive activities rather than waiting for something to happen (Rutter, Maughan, Mortimore, Ouston, & Smith, 1979).

These teachers keep all students actively engaged because they have high expectations for all students. It's easy to spot such teachers. They don't "write kids off" because of student background or attitude. They assume responsibility for teaching all students, not just those who want to learn. They are always looking for new ideas when old strategies no longer work. These expectations and attitudes create a "self-fulfilling prophecy" (Brothy & Evertson, 1981). If you believe a student can learn, you persist in teaching that student until the learning occurs!

Our expectations may determine who is actively participating in the classroom. This chapter will explore techniques for keeping all students involved through teacher questioning. This participation won't be achieved by just asking students more questions! Students already have between 3-5 questions fired at them per minute (Rowe, 1978). The secret lies in how teachers ask questions, to whom they are directed, and how teachers respond to student answers.

103

WHO IS TYPICALLY INVOLVED

Active participation in classroom activity is not fairly distributed. The students who probably need it the most experience it the least: low achievers. Think of those students in class you suspect are low achievers. Are they the same students who cause management problems? We may create this situation ourselves! In many cases, it is our expectations that these students are low achievers that determines their lack of opportunity to respond in the classroom (Cooper, 1979).

Teachers smile more often and nod their heads more if they perceive a student as bright. These same students are given more opportunity to respond in class and are given more positive and encouraging feedback than low achievers (Cornbleth, Davis, & Button, 1974). Pity the students for whom a teacher has low expectations:

-they are given less time to answer a question
-more call-outs are allowed if they should as much as pause in answering a question
-the teacher is less likely to elaborate on their answers
-even if their answer is correct, the astonished look on the teacher's face communicates low expectations

Is it any wonder, then, that these students find "bigger and better" things to do, probably not related to the task at hand?

It's easy to see how this self-fulfilling prophecy continues to be reinforced. The teacher asks a question—a few hands go up—teacher calls on someone. That someone is generally a bright student who knew the answer immediately. Or, the teacher uses a student's name at the beginning of the question: "Sia, can you tell me . . . ?" Unconsciously, we want students to have correct answers. It's easier to call on someone who has the right answer. It even makes us feel better as a teacher—reinforcement that we taught!

If a low achiever is called upon and gives an incorrect answer, it is a poor model for others to hear. The teacher must then take time to respond to the incorrect response. It's hard to be positive with a wrong answer! The momentum of the class is slowed down if reteaching of the same material must occur. How easy it is to move on to someone else who has the right answer—a high achiever! It might look like this:

Teacher: "What countries were involved at the start of World War II?"

Low expectation student: "Canada?"

Teacher: "No, Mike, you haven't been listening! Who has the right answer?"

High expectation student: "Germany, Great Britain."

Teacher: "Great, Rollo. I knew you could do it!"

One questioning strategy heard consistently at all grade levels begins with: WHO CAN TELL ME . . . This *who can tell me* preface to our questions subtly reveals expectations: some students will have the answers, some won't. One can't help wondering if those students who have a low academic self concept just tune out the questions entirely as soon as the cue *who can tell me* is given.

Cooper (1979) has developed a model describing the effects of teacher expectations on student performance:

1. Teachers have different expectations for student performance—depending upon ability and background.

2. Teachers find that when low expectation students respond, they have less control over student responses and the interaction is less likely to end successfully.

3. Low expectations students therefore face a more negative climate. They are criticized for control purposes.

4. Low expectations students decrease participation rates in class; they are less likely to respond. They develop the belief that the teacher, not their effort, determines success.

5. A self-fulfilling prophecy has begun.

TECHNIQUES TO CREATE
EQUAL PARTICIPATION

Understanding the dynamics of the cycle may be enough to change unequal treatment of students. Good and Brophy (1974) found that just giving feedback to teachers about their behavior caused them to increase their contacts with low expectation students. Just this change in teacher behavior resulted in lows seeking more contacts with teachers and a tendency for them to be better behaved.

105

Randomization

To insure that expectations aren't influencing who is called upon in a class, we need a technique to guarantee randomness. Examples might include:

1. Have a can of popcycle sticks, each with the name of a student. When a question is asked, draw a stick to see who to call upon. Students soon learn that raising their hand isn't the determiner of who's called upon. They also learn that the teacher isn't picking favorites or just plain "picking on someone" (for management purposes).

2. Some secondary teachers have a deck of 3 x 5 cards with a student name on each card. They shuffle the deck at the beginning of each period. Some even record on the card whether the student attempts to answer the question. They then have a fairly accurate record of class participation.

3. When several students are needed for board work, use the "army style selection" process. Select (or have students select) a random number from 1 to 10. If the number is three, point randomly to class list and call out every third name!

The random selection technique has a double edge to it. Students know in advance they are likely to be called upon—they're more likely to be listening. Teachers, knowing they have an equal chance of calling on a low, may provide better instruction before asking the question—to avoid having to handle an incorrect response!

Wait Time

Rowe (1978) found that just calling on lows more often isn't enough. The "I don't know" or "No" response was often as high as 30% in normal classrooms. She found that teachers could change this lack of responding pattern of lows by adding "wait time" after asking a question and waiting after a student response. That is, the teacher asks a question and waits about three seconds before calling on a student. The student responds and again the teacher waits before reacting. For example:

"I want all of you to think of the author's point in the story."
3 SECOND WAIT

"John, what do you think?"

John answers"............................."

3 SECOND WAIT

Teacher reaction/response

Rowe found teachers and students alike were affected by the wait time. Outcome variables particularly relevant to increasing active participation by all included:

1. Length of student response increased.
2. Number of unsolicited but appropriate responses by students increased.
3. Failure to respond decreased.
4. Confidence in responding increased.
5. Contributions by "slow" students increased.
6. Disciplinary moves decreased. Without wait time there was more restlessness, inattentiveness, and unsocial behaviors.

In addition to wait time, subtle changes in how the teacher phrases questions help increase active participation. Consider the difference between the following two questions:

1. What is the difference between a noun and a pronoun?
2. Think about the difference between a noun and a pronoun. Raise your hand when you're ready with your answer.

In the first example the teacher is likely to get a "blurter-outer": an eager responder who deprives the rest of the class of their chance to think of the answer. The lower the level of the question (i.e. calling for a rote recall type answer), the more likely someone is to blurt out —- unless

1. The question is phrased to encourage thinking.

2. Students are told what signal to use to cue the teacher they are ready with an answer.

The following patterns demonstrate both characteristics:

-Take a moment and imagine that . . . Raise your hand when you're ready.

-Pretend that . . . Look up at me when you can tell me.

-Think to yourself . . . Thumbs up when you're ready to respond.

107

-Consider for a minute . . . I'll call on a non-volunteer for an answer.

GROUP RESPONDING

Group responding is another technique to consider in maintaining momentum and accountability. While the research is limited and mixed on the benefits of group responses over individual responses, it would seem logical to try any technique to get low achievers involved in the lesson. Group response is a way to hold everyone accountable for being on task and gives the teacher opportunity to monitor the understanding of the whole class—not just a selected few. It should also encourage more learning if all students have to mentally process information. This recitation gives students practice in retrieving information, necessary for effective learning (Higbee, 1977).

Simply asking for a group response may not accomplish the benefits described. Unless the teacher can cue students to respond in unison, a ripple response occurs. For example, when asking "What is 7 x 9?", a few eager students blurt out "63" and a fraction of a second later the less eager echo "63". The "echoers" haven't had to rehearse retrieving information; only listen to their peers. Likewise, when the question calls for a finger signal, "How many syllables in family?", a few three-finger hands begin waving. They provide the model for the remainder of the class to copy.

A better guarantee that everyone has thought of the answer when asking for a group response is to give a cue for response in unison. "When I nod my head, you may answer."

GROUP TECHNIQUES

Choral responding is fast, efficient, and requires no extra materials. It allows all students to respond anonymously. The drawback is that the teacher only gets a general reading on the ability of the class to answer. It is difficult to monitor specific students. It's also limited to questions demanding a low level, rote type response. Teacher: "Is an alder an evergreeen or deciduous tree?" Class: "Deciduous." Choral responding wouldn't work if multiple single word answers or complete statements are required. A question like "What is an example of a proper noun?" could be changed to allow only one response: "Which is a proper noun—cat or Garfield?" Younger students are often taught to whisper the answer to eliminate the tendency to shout out answers.

Choral responding keeps students on their toes without interrupting the momentum and pacing of the instruction. It sometimes sounds like a *fill in the blanks lecture.* "Class, today we'll study the knee joint. You'll remember that another name for joint is _____ what? Yesterday we learned that the two bones below the femur are the tibia and _____ what?"

Signals are similar to choral responding in that they are efficient and require no extra materials. Signals include the use of thumbs, fingers, pointing, and gesturing to indicate an answer.

After selecting one student to respond, the rest of the class might be asked if they agree (thumbs up), disagree (thumbs down); or not sure (thumb sideways). Used occasionally, this technique works. However, when every teacher at a middle school I visited recently, used this strategy repeatedly — the results were far from successful. By the time students reached their 7th period class, some students were observed with a hand in a "thumbs up" position throughout the lesson! A perfect cover while they engaged in other off-task behavior!

Finger signals can be used to indicate numerical answers or "choice type" answers. It is most effective when students are taught to signal with hand against chest. This eliminates the ripple effect of students in the first row advertising the answer to all sitting behind. "Show me how many tens are in 47." "Show me how many teaspoons are in a tablespoon." "I'll name a food. You signal 1 if in the meat group; 2 if dairy; 3 if vegetables or fruit; 4 if grain." Multiple choice questions lend themselves to any subject as well as all grade levels.

Individual chalkboards have always been popular at the primary grades to engage all students. Children bring old socks from home to use as a mitt for erasing. A similar technique for older students is to provide "think pads".

" . . . more effective teachers arranged their classrooms and planned activities that allowed them to monitor their students more easily and more thoroughly."

Evertson & Anderson, 1979

Old or non-usable worksheets are cut into fourths and a pad of them stapled at the corner. These small scratch pads remain on the corner of each student desk—for easy accessibility. "Try to solve this equation on your think pad." "Write a sentence showing possession." Teachers may either walk around and monitor work or have students hold up their pad. Some secondary students seldom remember to bring note paper to class and don't want to use their precious paper for practice when they finally do bring it. Think pads avoid this problem. Plastic lids (i.e. from a Cool Whip or other plastic container) can be used as a handy writing pad. Crayon writing can be seen from the front of the room easily and can be wiped off with a small piece of Handi-Wipe cloth. "Class, draw a right triangle on your lid. Now, FLIP YOUR LIDS!"

Sharing answers with a neighbor gives everyone a chance to verbalize a more complex answer. As students are explaining to a peer, the teacher can walk around and monitor particular students. It's important that desks or tables be arranged to allow maneuverability. Many times our students in the back two corners of the room are the most likely to be off task—and the least likely to be monitored! "Describe the events leading up to the Industrial Revolution to someone sitting close to you. I'll be around to listen."

If we are making *quality* use of time, we must be sure to include more than rote recall type questions.

If each and every student has to *construct* an answer, we also increase comprehension of the lesson. Effective strategies during a lesson would be to have all students:

> relate lesson to own experiences
> give an example, analogy, or metaphor
> draw inferences
> explain in own words
> give a summary

Students won't do this spontaneously by themselves. The teacher must ask the question and allow time for the processing to occur.

GROUP RESPONDING TECHNIQUES

whisper
fingers
arm is giant pencil: write in air
"mouth" it (non-verbal)
close eyes—signal
nod
thumbs up/down/sideways
write on lid/scratch paper
write on arm (magic finger)
point in direction
close your eyes if the answer is . . .
whisper to the person next to you
discuss with your neighbors
form punctuation with your hand (. , ! , ?)

Below are typical reading group questions. The questions can be restructured using techniques for active participation described above:

1. Who can read this word?
2. Who was your favorite character in the story?
3. Who can find an example of courage in the story?
4. Who can give me an example of their own?

Notice the difference:

1. When I point to the word, all of you whisper it.
2. Tell the person next to you who your favorite character was in the story.
3. Everyone find one example of courage in the story. Point to it with your marker.
4. All of you think of your own example of courage. Look at me when you have it.

SUMMARY

Given the choice, many students would choose to follow the law of least effort. That is, they will put no more effort into the lesson than is required of them. When teachers offer this opportunity to tune out a lesson — by calling on only the eager or high achievers — the potential for management problems increases. Questioning students consistently — not eventually — during the lesson increases their active participation in the learning and decreases their opportunity to be off task. High expectations for achievement, a characteristic of effective schools, is reflected in our questioning of students.

CHAPTER 9
Motivation and Minority Students

Educational research in the '70s focused on increasing learning gains. Competencies in diagnosis and prescription were listed as characteristics of effective teachers. The whole process resembled the doctor-patient relationship. Unfortunately, there is a big difference. The patient wants to be well and will welcome the prescription. Students, instead, react to the prescription with

"Do I have to?"

"BORING!"

Students don't passively receive instruction. The teacher, therefore, is challenged with the task of getting the attention of students. How can teachers motivate students to attend to instruction? This chapter will focus on those variables, under the control of the teacher, that will increase the focus (motivation) of minority students, in particular.

"The poor school performance of the Chicano, black, or American Indian child is thought to relate to membership in these social or cultural groups, and particularly to motivational problems that ensue with such membership" (Maehr, 1978). Social and cultural factors only influence motivation . The proactive teacher will USE this information to devise motivational strategies whereas the reactive teacher will simply use this group membership as an excuse for the inability to motivate minorities.

Frequently threats and shame have been used to motivate students. "You won't pass if you don't study for this test." "You'll have to make up time after school if you don't get to work." Anxiety will motivate some students—not all students. In fact, with minority students creating anxiety may have the opposite effect in comparison with the effect on mainstream youth. This chapter will examine some other techniques that may be more appropriate for increasing motivation in minority youth: success, knowledge of results, interest, and level of concern.

The process-product research of the '70s looked primarily at the implications of simple two variable relationships. For example, teacher criticism is negatively related to pupil achievement. But, this relationship is modified by the influence of a third variable: student characteristics. Mild criticism may be positive for pupils with higher academic orientation, negative for pupils with lower academic orientation (Gage, 1978). Minority children are particularly sensitive to criticism. Similarly, many generalizations describing teacher techniques that increase motivation or focus may be modified when the third variable, membership in a minority group, is added. Thus, while the variables of success, knowledge of results, interest, and level of concern have been found to increase the attentive behavior of students, how will the relationship change when the variable of minority status is added?

SUCCESS

The most motivated student in the classroom is likely to be academically successful. The least motivated is likely the learner who has experienced repeated failure. We can predict who these failing students will be in the primary grades. By the end of second grade, two-thirds of the children who will be failing in arithmetic in grade six can be identified on the basis of socio-economic data, intelligence test scores, and an arithmetic achievement test (Stodolsky & Lesser, 1967). Add to this Bloom's research (1981) that shows by the end of the third grade, 50% of the variation at grade 12 can be accounted for. Armed with such diagnostic precision, just think how proactive we can be in preventing this failure cycle from occurring!

Mastery learning "is the most logical place to begin if we are going to assure children of success experiences"

(Vasquez, 1978). Mastery philosophy suggests that given enough time and proper learning conditions, all children can learn the objectives we set out to teach them. Instead of teaching content, we are teaching children! Mastery techniques include diagnosing specific learning needs, prescribing appropriate materials, and providing correctives when initial instruction is not effective. The identification of a clearly defined objective and the performance standard necessary for mastery lets students know that they will be judged on what THEY accomplish, not how they compare with their peers (as grading on the normal curve causes).

Crucial to being able to provide a productive learning climate in which mastery teaching can occur is the teacher's classroom management skills. The setting of expectations, teaching of rules, and establishment of control were found to be the biggest differences between successful and less than successful teachers in low SES minority schools (Moskowitz & Hayman, 1976; Sanford & Evertson, 1980). Less effective teachers allow discipline problems to escalate until many students are out of hand and then try to stop them with threats. Effective teachers use less class time reacting to discipline problems while less effective teachers use considerably more. With the current research emphasizing the importance of time on task for successful learning, management skills are definitely a prerequisite to mastery learning techniques. The techniques described in this book particularly important for teachers of minority students include:

-significant portions of class time devoted to discussion and review of rules and procedures during first three weeks of school
-consistent enforcement of rules
-allowing students to experience early success
-instructional activities filling class time (no dead time)
-opening class and dismissal time routines established
-staying in charge of all of the students, all of the time
-clear directions given; no student confusion

Success And Clear Directions

The ability to give effective directions is a skill that needs particular emphasis not only for maintaining a productive learning environment but also for allowing students to experience success in learning content. A student's failure on tasks may be due not to lack of understanding of content, but failure to understand directions for completion of task. The section on effective direction giving in Chapter 4 is particularly applicable here.

Success And Locus Of Control

Students have different ideas about what causes success or failure. Psychologists refer to this as locus of control. For example, success on a task may be attributed to ability and effort (internal locus of control) or to the difficulty of the task or luck (external locus of control). Achievement motivation is a function of the degree of internality in locus of control. Yet, minority students tend to score as externals on locus of control tests (Vasquez, 1978). They are more likely to say "The teacher gave me a bad grade," rather than "I didn't know the answers to the questions."

We need techniques to increase the internal attributions of minority students. Effective direction giving, proactive management strategies, and mastery learning techniques can provide the success that minority students need to experience to increase their internal locus of control and consequently, their motivation to learn. Their success on immediate tasks is likely to transfer to an expectancy of success on future tasks. This perception of competence may lead to a generalized internal locus of control. Clearly established rules and routines let the student know she can choose to be a part of a productive learning atmosphere—not subject to the whims of the teacher. Step by step directions allow a student to assume responsibility for completing assignments and not feel dependent on the teacher for guidance. Behavioral objectives that are prescribed for students in small incremental steps allow for success and internal attribution of ability. One's own effort determines mastery, not how one compares with the rest of the class. Success so defined is within the control of the student.

KNOWLEDGE OF RESULTS

Providing a student with feedback about the adequacy of her response helps the student focus on the task. The recommendation for appropriate use of knowledge of results as a motivator is that they be immediate and specific. "Knowledge of results is when students know within one hour correctness of responses" (Popham, 1973). "Research indicates that knowledge of results is more effective when it contains information about what the correct response should be, rather than merely letting the student know he is wrong" (Anderson & Faust, 1973).

Translation of these generalizations into practice with minority students may require refinement in light of what we know about locus of control. The reinforcement a student experiences when finding out her response is correct contributes to the feeling of success and motivation. Students with an internalized locus of control may provide that reinforcement themselves. Minorities, who tend to be more external, may not. They may attribute feedback on their success as just luck or an easy task. Even with clear directions, their lack of self reliance may cause them to lean on the teacher for assistance in completing assignments. Their eventual success on the task is attributed to outside help.

Achievement motivation is increased if feedback includes encouragement for students to make:
-internal attributions of ability and effort for success
-and, lack of effort attributions for failure (Bar-Tal, 1978).

Children given this type of feedback show greater task persistence and improved performance when compared to students not receiving such training. For the classroom teacher, then, strategies might include:

-Send answer sheet home so student can correct own homework, record time spent and why such a score was received

-"You spent the entire period working on your problems and you got them all correct. Great job!"

-"Your topic sentence is right on! You need to work on your supporting sentences. Try one sentence at a time and then bring it to me and we'll check it together."

-Student misses problem, teacher provides additional instruction . . . "You solve the next problem while I stand and watch . . . great! You don't need my help any more."

Providing students immediate and specific knowledge of results and attributing results to student's own effort seems relatively easy to implement in classrooms. Research, though, indicates that such may not be the case. Minority students make up a disproportionate percentage of the low achievers in our classrooms. And, students perceived as low achievers receive inferior treatment by teachers. "Instead of providing lows with at least equal attention, assistance, and support, teachers tended to neglect them" (Cornbleth, Davis, & Button, 1974).

MEANING
What teacher hasn't been admonished to "make the lesson meaningful" to students? Meaning can be created by:

-taking items that may be nonsense to the learner and hooking them to something the learner is already familiar with

-organizing or building pattern into the learning

-identifying logical relationships; explaining how concepts are alike and different

-giving the purpose for the lesson; how the skill may be used

Before the teacher can make that lesson meaningful, the teacher must also know something about the lives of the students in the class: language used, interests, how spare time is spent, value system. Knowing this can help in the building of mental bridges to touch the students' lives. Without this, one can become "the teacher who teaches whether or not the student is learning" (Postman & Weingartner, 1969).

The amount of meaning derived from a passage is related to the frequency of word usage of each of the individual words in that passage. Think of the barriers this sets up for many minority students! The following passage was taken from a junior high math text:
"We say that a polynomial has been completely factored if each of the factors is prime. The binomial 2x-3 is prime is we restrict ourselves to integers as coefficients."

Without translating this passage into vocabulary more consistent with the language used daily by the student, the meaning of it is lost.

Psychologists have identified a learning style construct (field dependence-independence) that helps describe learning styles and can assist the teacher in providing meaning for students. The Mexican-American student has many characteristics of the field dependent learner (Multilingual Assessment Project, 1972). Field dependents are better at learning material containing human content and need to know how classroom activities can help other people. These types of examples should be provided during instruction. They also have greater difficulty in learning material that lacks clear inherent structure (Witkin, Moore, Goodenough, & Cox, 1977). Teachers can assist by providing outlines, advance organizers, or concise summaries of the material. Programmed learning materials with their inherent step by step structuring help field dependent learners.

Knowledge of use or purpose is particulary important for our minority students. While they have the ability to achieve at higher levels—they just DON'T. "The overriding factor explaining why these young people are not reading is motivation, or lack of it. Many of these young people simply are not aware of the need to learn to read" (Project Read, 1979). Techniques specific to the area of reading for providing that "need" might include the development of functional learning packets using:

forms (job application; application for social security card; telephone application; doctor's form; ordering from a catalog)

labels (aspirin, suntan lotion, food labels)

advertisements (coupons, cars, clothing)

magazines

reference material (inside cover of telephone book, area code map, table of contents, long distance call guide)

LEVEL OF CONCERN

Level of concern is that fear of losing something you need or want (love, affection, status, success, esteem, etc.) It's that worry one feels before giving a speech, before taking a test, or when the teacher calls on you and you don't have the answer. It's also like medication when you're ill. Without it you won't get any better, with too much you'll really be sick. Only with the right dosage will you get well. The question now is, how do we find the right dosage of level of concern for minority students?

The design of the traditional classroom probably creates too high a level of concern for minority students and consequently does not function as a motivator. The design is the competitive atmosphere that promotes that fear of losing. Students are asked to compete for grades, on tests, for privileges, for any recognition! Mexican-American children achieve best through activities that promote cooperation in contrast with the Anglo-American's competitive nature (Kagan, 1980). Aronson (1980) found that blacks and Mexican American students learned much more in cooperative classes than in competitive classes.

While many of the techniques suggested so far to motivate minority students require only a refinement of teacher instructional skills, the change to a cooperative classroom may require a major overhaul. Considerable research is available to provide models for teachers. Slavin (1980) has researched three strategies (STAD, TGT, and Jigsaw Two) and found increased learning gains for minority students. Aronson (1980) developed a strategy, Jigsaw, that also promotes the cooperative social orientation of minority children. The concerned teacher will be on the lookout for any strategy that fosters helping others, avoiding both subordination and dominance, and the chance to achieve gains and avoid losses for the group. (See Chapter 6: Learning in Cooperative Groups)

One of the school's competitive situations causing high level of concern—that of taking tests—can be altered gradually by teachers. Research has shown that high test-anxious people respond more positively to reassurance, modeling cues, persuasion, and conformity pressures (Tryon, 1980). Specific strategies include:

-many frequent quizzes (so that anxiety doesn't build up and create debilitating effects)

-let students contribute questions for test

-give test questions out ahead of time

-let students bring to test a 3x5 card on which they have written any prompts they choose

-begin test with easy questions/problems to insure experience of early success

-teach study skills to students

-model the use of good practice theory by building in short, frequent practice periods during class for students

-try relaxation exercise before test

Special emphasis needs to be placed on relaxation for more than just test taking situations. Recent research has emphasized relaxation as a general skill for coping with anxiety (Tryon, 1980). Strategies such as role playing, visualization, special use of music, as well as relaxation have been found to affect student motivation as well as student beliefs about his own ability to learn (Prichard & Taylor, 1980).

SUMMARY
While human beings are sensitive to many variables as motivators, this chapter has examined four (success, knowledge of results, meaning, and level of concern) as they relate to minority students. The purpose was to look at cultural differences as question marks, not periods. That is, how can these differences be used to devise motivational strategies for minority students?

CHAPTER 10
Brain Research and Teaching

Critics in the '60s said schools weren't doing their job. They offered many suggestions for improvement. . . . suggestions that were considered radical by many educators. Ironically enough, recent brain research lends credibility and a sense of urgency to those "radical" suggestions. Educators in the '80s are now faced with implementing these changes.

What did the critics say? That formal education is dominated by an emphasis on the machine and engineering principles. That schools mirror the philosophy of an extremely rational and cognitive society—prescribing that the ideal citizen should be a literate, analytic person (Quigley, 1968). That students who can't fit the system turn to the occult, Free University, classes in Eastern thought, oriental art, psychedelic paraphernalia and communes. That kids are spending billions of dollars on LP records and to see films as another source of aesthetic experience not provided by our literary minded schools (Postman, 1972).

Educators themselves must have sensed an imbalance. Moves toward objectives, accountability, and criterion reference testing have flourished. Critics, however, see this as concentrating on the wrong solutions to the wrong problems in the wrong places! Weingartner (1972) makes this point vividly with the comment "I should ask that we have about two seconds of silence for the statistician who drowned while wading across a river with an average depth of three feet."

It is the same old story—the very tools educators use to remedy the situation are the same tools that created the situation: rationality, reductionism, and the philosophy that there is one right answer for every question. Shane

(1973) comments that if the move towards accountability and behavioral objectives continues, it will lead to a "new breed of computer-oriented or didactic teachers." While we may not know for **sure** what needs to be done, there have been many suggestions.

RESEARCH ON THE BRAIN

Recent research on the brain may cause us to reconsider how we traditionally spend our time in classrooms. The description of the structure and operation of this three pounds of matter moves us closer to a true science of teaching and learning.

The brain is described vertically as consisting of the reptilian complex (controlling circulation, respiration, consciousness); the limbic system (controlling emotional behavior, glandular functions, and maintaining homeostasis); and the neocortex (processing sensory information and problem solving). The left/right horizontal description of the neocortex interests educators as this controls higher mental functions.

Research has shown that physiologically the human cortex has two hemispheres and that psychologically each has its own mode of perception. The first evidence of specialization came from studies of brain lesions. Stroke or accident victims who suffered impairment in the right hemisphere have difficulty with spatial arrangement, detecting emotion and humor in reading, three-dimensional vision, and even facial recognition. In contrast, patients suffering impairment to the left hemisphere have problems with reading, writing and arithmetic.

Roger Sperry continued this line of work with patients subject to epilepsy. In an effort to curb seizures, the bundle of nerve fibers (corpus callosum) connecting the two hemispheres was cut. Resultant experiments with these split brain patients showed that once separated the two hemispheres were operating independently of one another. If information was received on one side, the other side was totally unaware of it. The different perceptual roles of each hemisphere were evident. Dr. Sperry was awarded the Nobel Prize in medicine and physiology in 1981 for his outstanding contribution.

Researchers have continued working with subjects with

no impairment. Electrodes placed on the brain reveal which hemisphere is most active while the person is performing certain tasks. If told to write a letter, the left hemisphere is most active; if asked to work on a jigsaw puzzle, the right hemisphere is most active. Other experiments (i.e. dichotic listening studies, visual half-field tests) have revealed similar lateralization. In almost all right handers and the majority of left handers, the specialization looks like this:

LEFT HEMISPHERE: speech (particularly verbs and abstract nouns), phonetic reading, rational cognition, sense of time, sequence, converging on a logical answer, analysis of parts of a whole, linear.

RIGHT HEMISPHERE: intuition, spatial relationships, holistic reasoning, orientation in space, artistic endeavor, crafts, integration of many inputs at once, facial recognition.

Although functions may be localized to a certain extent, the other half of the brain is not totally silent. Reading, for example, is thought to combine word recognition (left) with structuring meaning (right). It's the orchestration of all parts of the brain that leads to memory and complex thought. Memory for any experience — verbal or visual spatial — is thought to be regulated through yet another part of the brain — the limbic system. It's becoming increasingly clear that the ultimate complexity of the brain is yet to be identified.

A growing understanding of the brain and evidence of individual learning styles has led to considerable speculation regarding educational practices. The implications for education suggested by brain researchers sounds very similar to the educational critics of the '60s:

Educators need to develop "sophisticated ways to facilitate the multiple processing systems of the brain" (Wittrock, 1977).

Learning will be optimum if teaching is to both hemispheres (Bogen, 1977).

" . . . normal brains are built to be challenged, that they only operate at optimal levels when cognitive processing requirements are of sufficient complexity to activate both sides of the brain and provide a mutual facilitation between hemispheres as they integrate their simultaneous activities" (Levy, 1983).

Students will feel frustration and hostility if they are forced to solve problems verbally, when they learn best with visual-spatial cues (Gazzaniga, 1977).
"Our educational system may miss training or developing half of the brain, but it probably does so by missing out on the talents of both hemispheres" (Springer & Deutsch, 1981).

Inferences have been drawn linking student misbehavior in the classroom to hemispheric preferences. Vitale (1982) believes the following are characteristics of right-hemispheric children:
appears to daydream
draws pictures on the corners of homework papers or dittos
has difficulty following directions
makes faces or uses other forms of non-verbal communication
is on the move most of the time
likes to work part-way out of seat or standing up
often has a messy desk
has difficulty in completing work on time
displays impulsive behavior
likes to touch, trip, or poke when relating to other children
goes to the pencil sharpener often

We await future research to confirm these speculations.

WHOLISTIC APPROACH TO LEARNING
If we aren't doing our job, as the critics of the '60s suggest, and we need to unleash the potential of the brain, what specifically should we do? The "critics" — before the impact of brain research — suggested:
- Make film making, picture taking, televising, computer-programming, listening, music playing, drawing and dancing the keystone of education (Postman, 1972).
- Develop the full sensory-perceptual capacities of

students with song, dance, language, storytelling, poetry, and social interaction.

-Help students "develop an environmental awareness . . . . practice an environmental ethic . . . . understand the characteristics of a global steady state system . . . " (Boyer, 1974).

Add to the curriculum an emphasis on environmental destruction, urban blight, social and racial tensions, poor mental health, and international conflict that threatens to lead to nuclear annihilation (Quigley, 1968).

-Value the intuitive and affective (Coppedge, 1972).

-Offer alternatives to the traditional classroom: community resources like courts, legislatures, community action groups (Scribner, 1972).

Researchers and educators working with our new understanding of the brain offer similar suggestions:

-Provide wholistic learning activities involving the body (i.e. dance, movement); mind (i.e. daily guided imagery practice, values awareness); emotions (feelings); and spirit (i.e. meditation) (Galyean, 1980).

-Incorporate right brain techniques in reading: learn concepts by direct or vicarious experience; learn vocabulary by having students form mental images (Fox, 1979).

-Rely less on words and formulas in lectures; begin to use both gesture and pictures to communicate with the nonverbal side of the student (Blakeslee, 1980).

As with all "revolutions" in education, there is the risk of substituting an emphasis on verbal, analytical approaches to education with an overemphasis on intuition and visualization. The key to educational reform will be to develop the potential of the brain. We can be misled by our intuition just as we can fail to find a solution to a problem using pure logic.

Research is just beginning to examine how to make full use of the specialities of the mind. It could be argued that traditional classroom teaching has always been supplemented with multi-sensory activities: field trips to museums and other community resources, laboratory experiences in science, role playing in social studies, and specialists in art and music. It could also be argued, though, that these activities were only supplements—not integrated with classroom instruction.

One recent study (Mackenzie & White, 1982) demonstrated the power of this integration for long term retention of instruction. Three different methods of instruction were used with secondary students in learning geography:

1. classroom instruction: a written program, including pictures

2. classroom instruction plus a "traditional" fieldtrip

3. classroom instruction plus a fieldtrip to the same location but different experiences. This fieldtrip had students using all senses to interact with the environment: walking through mudflats, tasting foliage for salinity, etc. Students became active, not passive, participants by recording information and asking/answering questions at the site. The students in the last group demonstrated much greater retention of information 12 weeks after the experience.

Perhaps what we learn from studies such as this is that what we need is not just more activities but more information on how to integrate and synthesize them. Acknowledging the need for research in this area, an attempt will be made to describe a more wholistic approach to typical classroom activities.

TEACHING

PRETEST
A pretest is NOT defined as a paper/pencil test! Teachers gain considerable diagnostic information from simply observing students. Watch them in the lunch line—how well do they count money? Listen to them chat with one another, diagnose word usage. Read papers written for other subjects to diagnose language arts skills.

MENTAL SET/OBJECTIVE
Instead of giving the teacher's reason for learning something, arrange for students to find reasons of their own. This can be from their past experiences or a concrete experience at the beginning of the lesson. Imagina-

tion, intuition, and feelings about the experience can be expressed. Some examples:

-A middle school science teacher held up a cruet of vinegar and oil and asked the question "Have you ever been at a restaurant and wondered why the dressing had oil at the bottom, vinegar at the top?" Students talked about their experiences and hunches. The teacher explained that they would find out why the separation occurred in their new lesson on density.

-A high school business teacher began a unit with a short skit about a student applying for summer work. The script had a student doing poorly in an interview: lack of enthusiasm, bad manners, lack of preparation, etc. After the skit, students were asked if they were the employer, would they hire that student and why. Feelings were shared and the experience was tied to the new unit on seeking employment.

-Students were asked to close their eyes and try to visualize what was happening in two paragraphs the teacher was going to read. One paragraph began "You are about to begin eating. In front of you is a hamburger with mustard, lettuce, cheese. . . . " The other began "You are anxious to begin eating. In front of you is a juicy hamburger smothered with tangy mustard, crisp lettuce, melted cheese. . . . ." Students talked about which paragraph made them feel like eating...which caused the best movie in their mind. A reason was being "discovered" for using adjectives in written work.

Simulations, role plays, and visualization activities can engage the whole brain in a mental set.

INPUT/MODELING

Traditionally the teacher's role is thought of as the giver of information (input). The passing on of this "acquired knowledge" doesn't have to be through reading or listening. It can be visual (i.e. film, videotape), tactile ("hands on") or kinesthetic (i.e. role play). It can be inductive or deductive. Some examples:

Social Studies: Films, skits and visualization activities may accompany lecture and reading. Students can direct a movie in their mind while the teacher uses storytelling as a means of teaching:

"Picture yourself as a Native American child growing up in a coastal tribe one hundred years ago. You are waking up one morning, slide off your wooden bunk onto a floor of cedar shavings. As you look around your long house, several other families are also rising. You walk out of the cedar planked house facing the river, wondering what you'll do for the day. You could help your mom dry and smoke salmon for the winter months or you could go with your father on a whale hunt in the 60 foot canoe . . . "

Students can follow this exercise by reading in their text about the life style of coastal Indians.

The teacher might set up a concrete experience for students first, then label what happened. In teaching the advantages and disadvantages of various solutions of the world food problem, one teacher began by telling the class that each student would get an "A" for the day if the class could divide a piece of bread equally between all students. "Who wants to start dividing?" Several students reached for the bread. While one student began breaking the bread, the teacher "stole" a piece, commenting "I may not be the biggest person in this class, but I am the most powerful." At the end of the exercise, students compared this to nations trying to divide food equally among themselves—and the problems accompanying this solution.

Spelling: Phonics or the "sound it out" strategy works less than half of the time with the English language. Visualization strategies are a needed complement. The shape of the word can be modeled: health. Students can be asked to visualize missing letters: he__lth. Students can practice writing words on their arm. If students are asked to write a word several times, be sure they don't just copy it! Have them cover original word, try to write it again from visual memory, then uncover word and see if there is a match.

Reading/Literature: Ask students to stop after each paragraph and form a visual image of what happened in the paragraph. Role play stories; show how characters feel non-verbally; cartoon a story to show sequence. Show films

132

or video tapes of stories before having students read them. One student commented "I never would have been able to read Romeo and Juliet if I hadn't seen it on TV first!"

Math: Ask students to visualize story problems; draw diagrams to demonstrate what the problem is asking; try to role play problems. Manipulatives—common in the primary grades—almost disappear thereafter. Perhaps a visit to primary classrooms by secondary teachers would generate more ideas on multisensory math.

CHECK FOR UNDERSTANDING/GUIDED PRACTICE

Activities similar to those described above can be used when checking to see if students understand the lesson: draw, diagram, body movement, etc.

INDEPENDENT PRACTICE/GROUPS

Some energetic Ph.D. Candidate should undertake the task of counting how many worksheets or dittos students are expected to complete throughtout their academic careers. These worksheets are definitely a "one-sided" approach to practice—linear, sequential, writing. The options for student practice are limited only by our own imagination! Students can practice new material by trying it out...experimenting and manipulating materials. These activities may accompany workbook pages or supplant them:

-Construct a mobile of the food groups (or plants/animals; types of trees; etc.).

-Make a mural showing events leading up to a war (or the circulatory system; a part of speech; etc.).

-Make a collage from magazine pictures that demonstrates liquid/solid (or happy/sad; health food/junk food, etc.).

-Cut and paste with construction paper fractional equations $(1/2 + 1/3 = 5/6)$.

-Go on a treasure hunt around room or school to find examples of shapes (or, textures; man-made materials; shades of color; etc.).

SUMMARY

Any discussion of hemisphericity—the left-right division of our brain—can lead to "dichotomania". The focus, instead should be on the whole. The brain is infinitely more complex than the left-right cerebral specialization discussed. Researchers continue to add to our understanding of brain growth periods, emotional development and the unity or functioning of the whole brain.

Research on brain growth spurts has implications for what we teach students and when (Epstein, 1978). The suggestion is to teach new challenging material during the spurt (rapid growth in axon/dendrite connections) and practice during the plateau periods. It may be premature, however, to make curricular changes until more is learned about the precise relationship between learning and the growth spurt.

Studies showing a relationship between emotions and thinking suggest other future changes for education (MacLean, 1978). Can emotions generated in the limbic system block learning in the neocortex? Will it be necessary to first deal with a student's negative attitude or boredom before trying to teach that student?

The constant refinement and modification of what we know about the brain makes it difficult to prescribe specific educational practices. Yet, neuroscientists and educators alike would agree on one thing: quality teaching stimulates the whole brain!

CHAPTER 11
Measuring Quality And Quantity Time

Conclusion

You might be asking yourself "Where do I begin?" This is the question I hear most frequently from teachers in a management workshop. If only there were a specific answer! From the ideas shared in the book you have undoubtedly said to some "I'm doing that already." or "That's not a problem for me." It's the ideas to which you responded "I could use that one . . . " for which you need to develop a plan of action.

As you reflect on your management system, what kinds of things bother you or cause you stress? Management is probably one of the biggest causes of stress for teachers. One stress profile for teachers (developed by E. Pino) includes many items directly related to classroom management:

> interruptions
> discipline
> grading
> tardiness
> extra assignments
> lack of sufficient help
> lack of time
> lack of praise
> student not accepting responsibilities
> not enough supplies
> students being taken from class
> students not paying attention
> poor student attitude
> lack of student achievement
> students don't work well together

If any of these classroom events create stress, look back in the book for ideas to "solve" them. It may not be possible to eliminate the problem entirely, but you can change "distress" (stress affecting you adversely) to "eustress" (manageable stress). And, be sure to select only one improvement objective at a time. Once you've accomplished it, you're ready for the next one!

I've found that when teachers have a chance to get together and share ideas and concerns, it's also stress reducing. Sometimes we think we're the only one experiencing the problem. And, who knows, perhaps one of your colleagues will have a solution. The ideas shared in the book have been gleaned from the classrooms of effective teachers!

To stimulate reflection and discussion of the management ideas presented, examples of lessons have been included with discussion questions. The lessons are presented on the Interactive Teaching Map (see Appendix for source). We developed the map to capture both quality and quantity teaching during a lesson. As you read the description of how the map is interpreted, you'll find it a summary of what each of the chapters in the book have presented.

The Map is a coding form on which teacher behaviors critical to maximizing quality and quantity time on task are recorded on a minute by minute basis. The behaviors are categorized by the function they serve, e.g. assessment, guided practice, direction giving. Because the complexity of the teaching act can not be reduced to these few categories, the map also provides space for observers to record anecdotal notes. These notes describe the lesson specifically.

A completed Map graphically records how instructional time was spent during a lesson. It pinpoints trouble spots and diagnoses possible invitations to disruption. It provides groups of teachers a common vocabulary to discuss instruction since the categories are valid across curriculums. Teachers can use this information to make decisions about changing priorities for spending instructional time. (A model of the Map is on pages 138-139.)

CATEGORY DESCRIPTIONS

Pretest
This category measures how much of a class period is spent diagnosing students through written or oral pre-tests. Assessing students for the prerequisite skills for certain

learning tasks can significantly increase their achievement (Bloom, 1976). It helps the teacher to decide where to start the lesson and which students are likely to need the most help.

Before beginning a unit on parts of speech, an effective teacher would check to see which parts of speech students can already identify and use appropriately. Before beginning a unit on subtracting fractions, that same teacher would check to see if students know a numerator from a denominator. These checks can be short in length and could be scored in class.

Mental Set/Objective

Effective teachers identify the learning objective to be mastered, including what the students need to do to show that they have mastered the lesson. Teachers who do not specify what the students are to learn for a given lesson keep them guessing, often because the teacher has not clearly decided what the goal of the lesson is. Along with the objective of the lesson, the teacher should demonstrate or explain why it is important to learn the material and how it will help the student to understand it. If the teacher and students know specifically what is to be learned, both students and teachers can focus on making the most of the class period.

One third grade teacher simply said, "How many of you would like to never miss a subtraction problem again?" Most hands went up in the class. The teacher went on to explain that he was going to teach them a way to check their subtraction problems with addition. The kids now knew what they were going to learn as well as why it could help them. They had a mental set.

Input

This category records the time the teacher spends actually teaching new material to the class (e.g.explaining, giving examples). The time spent in input is effectively used when it targets the material the students need to know to achieve the objective. Unfortunately, it is not unusual to observe a teacher start a new lesson and immediately give students a worksheet on the material—leaving input out altogether.

If students are to learn the characteristics of the four

Minutes	Pretest	Mental Set/ Objectives	Input	Modeling	Guided Practice/ Check For Understanding	Independent Practice	Groups	Praise	Sponge/ Enrichment	Procedures/ Directions	Reactive Management	No Task Defined # Off Task
0												
1												
2												
3												
4												
5												
6												
7												
8												
9												
10												
11												
12												
13												
14												
15												
16												
17												
18												
19												
20												
21												
22												
23												
24												
25												
26												
27												
28												
29												
30												
31												
32												
33												
34												
35												

Instruction   Management

School	Date	Period	#Students	Conference Held	INTERACTIVE TEACHING MAP
				☐ Pre ☐ Post	Lesson Objective
Teacher		Observer			Conference Reinforcement Objective
Anecdotal Notes:					Refinement Objective

0	
1	
2	
3	
4	
5	
6	
7	
8	
9	
10	
11	
12	
13	
14	
15	
16	
17	
18	
19	
20	
21	
22	
23	
24	
25	
26	
27	
28	
29	
30	
31	
32	
33	
34	
35	

seasons, it is the teacher's responsibility to teach that first. Other interesting ideas and activities can be included if there is time left for them. An explanation of the equinox, discussion of favorite vacation spots during summer, and a dot to dot coloring ditto of a snowman might be motivating activities for students; but, if these activities take up most of the instructional time, students have lost the opportunity to spend time directly learning the characteristics of the four seasons.

Modeling

This category records the visual-spatial activities a teacher provides. Students learn better when they learn with all of their senses. Modeling might be the teacher showing how to solve a problem on the chalkboard or showing a sample of a finished product (i.e. letter) while naming the important parts. If the students can both see it and hear it, they are much more likely to remember it.

Guided Practice/Check for Understanding

Frequent checks to see if the students understand new material tell the teacher when to summarize, when to repeat, when to remediate and when to test. Checking on learning as it takes place provides opportunities for teachers to make these necessary adjustments. Just asking the question, "Do you understand?" will not tell the teacher if the learning has indeed occurred and the lesson can continue; instead, all it tells the teacher for sure is that students can nod their heads or give blank looks! Many students have mastered the art of sleeping with their eyes open! It is this constant interaction with students that has led researchers to describe effectiveness in terms of "active" (Good, 1979) and "interactive" teaching (Stallings, 1980).

Monitoring occurs while the lesson is going on, unlike the diagnostic quiz which occurs at the beginning of a new unit. It can be accomplished in a variety of ways:

-asking for signals ("Show me with the correct number of fingers how many syllables are in the word *practice".)*

-asking for a written response ("Jot down three causes of the American Revolution.")

-asking for choral responses from the group ("Class, tell me the capital of Oregon.")

The key to effective checking for understanding is that the majority of the class is sampled—not just students with their hands up. Otherwise, we fall into the trap of teaching to the best students and leaving the rest behind.

Independent Practice

This category measures the amount of time students spend working independently. Working alone on seatwork is a frequent activity in classrooms. While it is necessary to provide practice on new learnings, the engagement rate of students working alone is less as compared to teacher-led groups (Rosenshine, 1980). When kids are working alone, the teacher can average only two minutes per hour of direct contact with a student in a class of thirty. In fact, time spent working alone with only one student is negatively related to learning (Stallings, 1980).

Groups

Studies have shown that students working cooperatively in heterogeneous groups gain in both achievement and student social relationships (Johnson, Johnson, & Scott, 1978; Slavin, 1980). These techniques facilitate both basic skill type objectives as well as high level cognitive objectives. Strong and consistent effects on relationships between black, white, and Mexican-American students have been found.

Groups are generally comprised of 4 students balanced for ability level, sex, and race. The use of groups can provide additional time for guided practice through peer tutoring. The tutee can have more individual attention than is possible from the teacher alone and the peer tutor can learn the material with greater thoroughness through having to explain it to another student.

Praise

Praise has been found to be more frequent in effective schools (Rutter, Maughan, Mortimore, Ouston, & Smith, 1979). When praise is specific, it can teach the students what the teacher wants them to do. When praise is contingent on specific student behaviors, students learn when and how to perform certain tasks.

Praise such as, "You wrote a great topic sentence. It

lets me know what your essay is about and it captured my interest." will be more helpful to students than the phrase, "You did a nice job!" Or, "Thank you for raising your hand and waiting to be called upon." is more specific than "I like your good behavior." Specific praise encourages the student to repeat that behavior in the future.

Sponge/Enrichment

Having a short practice assignment on the board when students enter or providing explicit directions on what to do when finished with work may eliminate wasted "wait" time. If the teacher prepares brief assignments for students who finish their work early, their learning of the the lesson can be extended and enriched. If these times are not filled with productive activities, they can create the potential for more discipline problems.

Procedures/Directions

While it is necessary to pass out books, turn in papers and line up, time for these activities should be kept to a minimum. Smooth transitions from one activity to the next are characteristic of effective classrooms (Brophy & Evertson, 1976). Procedures such as getting ready for dismissal and taking roll can absorb large amounts of valuable time.

Managerial skills, in general, are strong determinants of learning (Good, 1979).If the class works frequently in small groups, the teacher should not have to take valuable time to explain the procedures each time—it should be a routine. For example, a flip of the light switch might be the signal to get into preassigned groups and begin work. If students turn in written work daily, a routine such as passing papers forward each time is much more efficient than changing the procedure or giving new directions every day.

Reactive Management

Frequent reactions to misbehavior are counterproductive to learning (Rutter et. al., 1979). Belittling, ridiculing, scolding, shouting, and criticizing are associated with low achievement (Tikunoff, 1975). Effective teachers proactively eliminate potential problems before they occur by anticipating them (Good & Brophy, 1978). Every instance of having to react or stop instruction to deal with management problems is time off task and contributes to an unpleasant feeling tone in the classroom.

Students will predictably be involved in minor misbehavior. The teacher has many options for dealing with these disruptions. By using the *Law of Least Intervention,* a positive feeling tone can be maintained and the misbehavior minimized. The *Law of Least Intervention* means that the teacher chooses the minimum disciplinary response to minor misbehavior which will stop it but detract as little as possible from instruction and the learning environment. For example, a young lady is combing her hair while the teacher is talking. One teacher might deliver a sermonette on when hair combing is appropriate. Instruction is interrupted and feelings are far from pleasant. Yet another teacher might simply continue teaching, walk over and stand by the student. The student is likely to put the comb away, the teacher can speak with her privately later, and no time is taken away from instruction.

No Task Defined

The amount of time students spend on task is directly related to achievement (Borg, 1980). When students are waiting for the teacher to begin, when they finish work early, or are waiting to leave, time for learning is lost. Announcements over the "squawk box" and visitors wandering through classrooms expecting to chat with teachers can also create this situation. This category clearly represents time away from learning.

EXAMPLES OF MAPPING TIME

Research has not revealed any ideal combination of teacher behaviors that is characteristic of effective classrooms. Similarly, there is no formula for how much time to spend on any one activity. Yet, it is possible to use a map of teacher behavior to analyze classroom interactions and keep track of how teaching time is used. The interaction of categories on the Map can be a specific diagnostic tool for identifying strengths and weaknesses.

Below are two examples of using the Interactive Teaching Map. They were coded during 35-minute observations of middle-school math classes. Notice the difference in quantity and quality of instructional time.

Minutes	Pretest	Mental Set/Objectives	Input	Modeling	Guided Practice/Check For Understanding	Independent Practice	Groups	Praise	Sponge/Enrichment	Procedures/Directions	Reactive Management	No Task Defined # Off Task
0									✔			
1									✔			
2									✔			
3									✔			
4									✔			
5									✔			
6		✔										
7		✔										
8		✔										
9			✔									
10			✔									
11				✔								
12				✔								
13				✔								
14					✔							
15					✔							
16					✔							
17					✔							
18			✔									
19			✔									
20				✔								
21				✔								
22					✔							
23					✔							
24					✔							
25					✔							
26					✔							
27					✔							
28										✔		
29							✔					
30							✔					
31							✔					
32							✔					
33							✔					
34							✔					
35							✔					

Instruction   Management

Every available minute was used for learning in this classroom. There were a variety of activities all directed toward a clearly defined learning.

School	Date	Period	# Students	Conference Held	INTERACTIVE TEACHING MAP
				☐ Pre ☐ Post	Lesson Objective
Teacher		Observer			Conference Reinforcement Objective
Anecdotal Notes:					Refinement Objective

0	(Teacher begins class by taking roll; students are solving review problems written on chalkboard.)
1	
2	
3	
4	
5	
6	We are going to learn how to find the average of a set of numbers. Let's list some of the times
7	you'll need this skill — both in and out of school. (Class discussion follows.) First, you need to
8	list the numbers you need to average in column form; then find the sum. Let me do a couple
9	of examples. First, the average age of boys in our class . . .
10	
11	
12	
13	
14	(Students are asked to set up problem to find average age of girls in class on a piece of
15	scratch paper; teacher walks around and checks.)
16	
17	
18	Next, you need to divide your sum by how many numbers you are averaging. Let me show you
19	with our example with the boys. Be sure to put the label too. In this case, it will be years.
20	
21	
22	(Students are asked to finish the problem begun with girls' ages; then solve one problem from
23	their text; teacher walks around to monitor work.)
24	
25	
26	
27	
28	We'll spend the remainder of the period in cooperative groups. Group leaders come up and get
29	your worksheet of problems. I'll come around to see how you are doing.
30	
31	
32	
33	
34	
35	

Next is a profile of another teacher's use of the 35-minute period of time.

Minutes	Pretest	Mental Set/Objectives	Input	Modeling	Guided Practice/Check For Understanding	Independent Practice	Groups	Praise	Sponge/Enrichment	Procedures/Directions	Reactive Management	No Task Defined # Off Task
0												✔
1												✔
2												✔
3												✔
4												✔
5												✔
6												✔
7										✔		
8										✔		
9										✔		
10			✔									
11			✔	✔								
12			✔	✔								
13				✔								
14											✔	
15											✔	
16												✔
17												✔
18												✔
19												✔
20											✔	
21										✔		
22										✔		
23						✔						
24						✔						
25						✔						
26						✔					✔	
27						✔						
28						✔					✔	
29						✔						
30						✔						
31												
32										✔		
33										✔		
34										✔		
35												

Instruction | Management

School	Date	Period	# Students	Conference Held	INTERACTIVE TEACHING MAP
				☐ Pre ☐ Post	Lesson Objective
Teacher		Observer			Conference Reinforcement Objective
Anecdotal Notes:					Refinement Objective

0	(Teacher begins class by taking roll. Students have nothing specific assigned. A few are chat-
1	ting; some out of seats; minor scuffle between two in corner.)
2	
3	
4	
5	
6	
7	Class, I need your attention now. Take out your math books. "I don't have one." "I forgot
8	mine, too." Alright, I'll look for some extras.
9	(Teacher looking for books.)
10	We'll work on rounding numbers to the nearest tenth. Let me show you . . .
11	
12	Now, let's round to the nearest hundred. (Several examples are shown on overhead projector.)
13	(Two students chatting in back of room.) Will you two turn around and save your discussion 'till
14	later? (Chatting continues while teacher teaches.) Okay. That's it. You two can make up time
15	after school. (Principal walks in to chat with teacher.)
16	
17	
18	
19	
20	You ought to be ashamed. You could have found something to do while I talked to Ms. Pratt.
21	Now, on page 69 you need to do the first fifteen problems. "Do we have to turn it in today?"
22	Yes. "Where do we put our work?" I'll collect it later. (Class works alone remainder of period.)
23	
24	
25	
26	Sh, sh. Keep it down.
27	
28	(Teacher asks disruptive student to sit by her.)
29	
30	
31	
32	May I have your attention now? Pass your papers forward. "I'm not done." You've had plenty
33	of time to finish. Your homework for tonight will be to finish the rest of the problems on page
34	69. You're excused.
35	

How much opportunity did this class have to learn? Some fast mental math shows that over 50% of the available time was not devoted to learning: no task defined, procedures, reactive. The teacher needs to convert more of that available time to productive learning. The following questions might be asked:

Could you have students work on a few practice problems while waiting for teacher to begin?

How could you have the rest of the class begin the assignment before finding additional books?

What questions might you ask that require group choral responding to perhaps eliminate chatting among students?

If you moved about the classroom while teaching, would your physical presence eliminate the chatting?

USING THE MAP

Teaching is demanding—teachers have an estimated 1000 interactions each day (Jackson, 1968). This demand does not leave time for the teacher to analyze how he is spending his time or if there are precious lost minutes that can be converted to learning time.

The Interactive Teaching Map and the ideas shared in this book can be used in a variety of ways to assist in finding TIME TO TEACH:

1. Using the Map as a form for structured feedback which teacher and observer may interpret together. From scanning the Map, teachers who are well versed in instructional strategies and classroom management techniques can identify what they may want to do differently.

2. Observers may use the Map as a basis for coaching teachers who are not knowledgeable in effectiveness research. The instrument adds objectivity to observers' suggestions for improvement. It also helps the observer to focus the observation and develops a common language for describing good instruction.

3. When Maps on several teachers in the building reveal similar needs, the map becomes a tool for diagnosing staff development needs. For example, if many minutes are lost to "no task defined", provisions might be made to pro-

vide an hour inservice on activities that can fill potentially wasted time.

4. One teacher taught her class about the Map and had them do Maps on her teaching! The feedback was helpful both to teacher and students.

5. With just a few hours of instruction on how to use the Map, teachers can begin observing one another. The Map serves to guide the observation and provide focus to the conference after the lesson. Teachers talking about good instruction and effective use of time are characteristics of effective schools (Little, 1981). Who knows, teachers may even volunteer to do a map on the principal during a faculty meeting. Who said time on task was for students only!

SELECTED LESSONS FOR ANALYSIS

The following lessons were selected to illustrate points made in each of the chapters of the book. Discussion questions are included to stimulate analysis.

Minutes	Pretest	Mental Set/ Objectives	Input	Modeling	Guided Practice/ Check For Understanding	Independent Practice	Groups	Praise	Sponge/ Enrichment	Procedures/ Directions	Reactive Management	No Task Defined # Off Task
0		✔										
1		✔										
2		✔										
3		✔										
4		✔										
5		✔		✔								
6				✔								
7				✔								
8				✔								
9										✔		
10					✔							
11					✔							
12					✔							
13					✔							
14					✔							
15					✔							
16					✔							
17			✔									
18			✔									
19												
20												

Instruction   Management

"Discipline . . . training that corrects, molds, or perfects the mental faculties or moral character."

Websters New Collegiate Dictionary

"Many of the more effective teachers had students write assignments daily on an assignment sheet to be kept in their notebooks."

Worsham & Evertson, 1980

School	Date	Period	# Students	Conference Held	INTERACTIVE TEACHING MAP
				☐ Pre ☐ Post	Lesson Objective
Teacher		Observer			Conference Reinforcement Objective
Anecdotal Notes:					Refinement Objective

0	Have you ever gotten your report card and found you received a lower grade in a class than
1	you expected? How did you feel? "Angry" "Upset" (etc.). What things could we do to prevent
2	that "surprise" at the end of the quarter? "Keep track of all of our grades on quizzes and
3	papers." Today I'm going to teach you how to keep a daily log of assignments and grades. It
4	will be your record of assignments, if you turned them in, and your grade. Let me show you
5	what it looks like (model on overhead). Here's how to record assignments.
6	
7	
8	Here's how to record your grade.
9	Paper monitors, please pass out record sheets.
10	Let me see how all of you would record today's assignment on the board. (Teacher walks
11	among desks, checking.)
12	
13	Now, paper monitors will return last week's reports. Show me how you would record both the
14	assignment and your grade. (Teacher monitors.)
15	
16	
17	We'll take the last few minutes of every class to maintain our records. Three times a quarter
18	you'll take them home for a parent signature.
19	
20	

DISCUSSION: In what way is teaching a management lesson similar to teaching academic material?

What could the teacher do to hold the students accountable for maintaining their log?

What will the benefits be from this lesson for both teacher and students?

Minutes	Pretest	Mental Set/ Objectives	Input	Modeling	Guided Practice/ Check For Understanding	Independent Practice	Groups	Praise	Sponge/ Enrichment	Procedures/ Directions	Reactive Management	No Task Defined # Off Task
0												✓
1												✓
2												✓
3												✓
4												✓
5										✓		
6										✓		
7			✓ alone									14
8			✓									
9			✓									
10			✓									
11			✓									16
12			✓									
13			✓									
14			✓									
15			✓									16
16			✓									
17			✓									
18			✓									
19											✓	
20												

Instruction | Management

"The most frequent ways new teachers met control problems were to ignore them and continue to teach or to wait until the situation was out-of-hand before trying to get order."

Moskowitz & Hayman, Jr., 1976

"Disillusionment with teaching is often the result of a lack of mastery of classroom management."

Spillman, 1980

School	Date	Period	# Students	Conference Held	INTERACTIVE TEACHING MAP
				☐ Pre ☐ Post	Lesson Objective
Teacher		Observer			Conference Reinforcement Objective
Anecdotal Notes:					Refinement Objective

0	(Teacher is late to class.)
1	
2	
3	
4	
5	(Directions for reading assignment given; most of class not listening.)
6	
7	(Students supposed to be reading. Those not reading: out of seat, chatting, throwing paper
8	wads.)
9	
10	
11	(Teacher makes no attempt to get quiet.)
12	
13	
14	
15	(Those trying to read complain it's too noisy.)
16	
17	
18	(Fight between two students breaks out.)
19	I've had it. You two are heading to the office.
20	

DISCUSSION: If this were your student teacher, where would you begin to establish better management?

How might this lesson be changed to encourage more student-teacher interaction?

Minutes	Pretest	Mental Set/ Objectives	Input	Modeling	Guided Practice/ Check For Understanding	Independent Practice	Groups	Praise	Sponge/ Enrichment	Procedures/ Directions	Reactive Management	No Task Defined # Off Task
0						✔				✔		
1						✔						
2						✔						
3						✔						3
4						✔						
5						✔						
6						✔						
7						✔						8
8						✔						
9						✔						
10						✔						
11										✔		
12						✔					✔	
13						✔						
14						✔						
15						✔						
16						✔						
17										✔	✔	
18	✔											
19	✔											
20	✔											
21	✔											
22	✔											
23	✔											
24	✔											
25	✔											
26	✔									✔		
27										✔	✔	7
28										✔		
29						✔						
30						✔						
31						✔						
32						✔						
33						✔						8
34						✔						

Instruction | Management

"Seatwork and students working alone is a dominant pattern. Overall students spend about 66% of their time doing seatwork during reading and about 75% of the time during math." **Rosenshine, 1980**

"In some less effective classes almost the entire period was given over to seatwork activities." **Emmer & Evertson, 1980**

154

School	Date	Period	# Students	Conference Held	INTERACTIVE TEACHING MAP
				☐ Pre ☐ Post	Lesson Objective
Teacher		Observer			Conference Reinforcement Objective
Anecdotal Notes:					Refinement Objective

0	I am going to set my timer. You have ten minutes for a "freewrite" in your journals. Let's keep
1	it quiet this time.
2	
3	
4	
5	
6	
7	(Chatting among students.)
8	
9	
10	
11	Alright, you've got five minutes to review your spelling list. Excuse me, Mandi. You know what
12	to do.
13	
14	
15	
16	
17	Close your books, please. Number 1 to 20. Sh. Sh. #1 — bacteria. Bacteria in food causes ill-
18	ness. #2 — routine. Our test is a once a week routine. #3 — centipede. A centipede has 100
19	legs.
20	
21	
22	(Spelling test continues.)
23	
24	
25	
26	Be sure your name is at the top. Pass your papers forward. Quiet please. There's too much
27	talking. You may work in your English books on p. 79. The directions are on the page. I'll
28	come around and help if you need it.
29	
30	
31	
32	
33	There'll be time to make up after school if I hear any more talking.
34	

"Much of what happens in classrooms today falls under the topic, 'allowing learning to occur'."
Anderson, 1982

DISCUSSION: Is the teacher teaching school or keeping school (facilitating learning vs. allowing learning to occur)? What can be added to this lesson to motivate students in the class?

Minutes	Pretest	Mental Set/ Objectives	Input	Modeling	Guided Practice/ Check For Understanding	Independent Practice	Groups	Praise	Sponge/ Enrichment	Procedures/ Directions	Reactive Management	No Task Defined # Off Task
0										✔	✔	
1		✔									✔	
2					✔						✔	
3					✔						✔	
4					✔						✔	
5										✔	✔	
6			✔ alone									
7			✔									
8			✔									
9					✔							
10											✔	
11												

Instruction | Management

"It is not advisable for teachers to intervene every time they notice a problem. Often, the disruptive effect of the teacher's intervention will be greater than that of the problem being dealt with."

Good & Brophy, 1978

School	Date	Period	# Students	Conference Held	INTERACTIVE TEACHING MAP
				☐ Pre ☐ Post	Lesson Objective
Teacher		Observer			Conference Reinforcement Objective
Anecdotal Notes:					Refinement Objective

0	Open your books to Chapter 7. David, get your arms in your sleeves. We'll work on the skill of
1	making inferences today. Jamal, did I say get your pencil out? All of you read the first
2	paragraph silently. Ryan, where does your money belong? What two steps will you use in mak-
3	ing inferences? Derek, you didn't raise your hand. Jeremy? Yes, examine the clues and make
4	an educated guess. I don't like the sounds I'm hearing, class. Now read the next paragraph.
5	I'll have you make an inference. (class reads) Excuse me, Rene, are you with us today?
6	(reading)
7	
8	(reading)
9	Who can tell me what season it is? Give me the clues, too. Derek "Spring . . . "
10	David, put your arms where they belong in your sweater, please.
11	

DISCUSSION: For each instance of reactive management, design an alternative for the "nagging reminder" that was used.
Was there any student behavior that could have been ignored?

Minutes	Pretest	Mental Set/ Objectives	Input	Modeling	Guided Practice/ Check For Understanding	Independent Practice	Groups	Praise	Sponge/ Enrichment	Procedures/ Directions	Reactive Management	No Task Defined/ # Off Task
0					1							
1					1							
2					1							
3					1							
4					1						✓	
5					1						✓	
6					1							
7					1						✓	
8					1							
9											✓	
10					1							
11					1							
12					1							
13					1							
14					1						✓	
15					1						✓	
16												

Instruction	Management

"Many schools are characterized by the assumption that their low SES and minority group students do not have the ability to learn and it would be inappropriate to demand that they do so."

Brookover et.al., 1979

158

School	Date	Period	# Students	Conference Held	INTERACTIVE TEACHING MAP
				☐ Pre ☐ Post	Lesson Objective
Teacher		Observer			Conference Reinforcement Objective
Anecdotal Notes:					Refinement Objective

0	Point to the hand at the top of the clock. What does it mean? Andy? "o'clock" Jason, what
1	does o'clock mean? "hand at top" Who will come up and write 2 numbers that mean o'clock?
2	Angie. Very good. What do the 2 numbers say, Zak? How many minutes are in one hour?
3	Mike? 60, good. I need someone to show the minute marks. Ali, go to 15. Now, Lyn, go to 30.
4	Sh. Sh. He is doing fine.
5	What do we say here? Mark? "5:30". Oh, someone blurted out an answer.
6	Mandi, no, not quarter after. We can say half past or 30 minutes past or 5:30. I want someone
7	to show me half past 4. Erico, good. Sh. Sh. You will all get a turn. Who can tell me two ways
8	to say this? Jan. "3:30 or half past 3".
9	Good. Oh, I can't call on you because I hear you. Sh.
10	Now, I need someone to come to the overhead and write the time you see on the this
11	clock. Jason.
12	Who can do this clock? Mary.
13	Raise your hand if you agree. Good. Now, the next clock?
14	Sh. Lisa, your hand is up.
15	Turn around please, Jacob. Mia, you may go up.
16	

DISCUSSION: Change each teacher question or activity to get more than one student involved in the lesson.

159

Minutes	Pretest	Mental Set/ Objectives	Input	Modeling	Guided Practice/ Check For Understanding	Independent Practice	Groups	Praise	Sponge/ Enrichment	Procedures/ Directions	Reactive Management	No Task Defined # Off Task
0		✔										
1		✔										
2		✔										
3		✔		✔								
4					all							
5				✔								
6				✔	all							
7				✔								
8				✔								
9				✔	all							
10				✔	all							
11				✔	all							
12				✔	all							
13					all							
14					all							
15												
16												
17												
18												
19												
20												
21												

Instruction   Management

School	Date	Period	# Students	Conference Held	INTERACTIVE TEACHING MAP
				☐ Pre ☐ Post	Lesson Objective
Teacher		Observer			Conference Reinforcement Objective
Anecdotal Notes:					Refinement Objective

0	Think of all of the times you might need to write down how much money you have or how
1	much something costs. "If we have a lemonade sale; sell our toys; make a Christmas list of
2	what we want," etc. What if we didn't know how to write the cost correctly — and put $30 for
3	lemonade instead of 30¢? "No one would buy any." We'll learn how to write amounts under a
4	dollar first. We will write this "¢" for the word cents. All of you try it on your think pad. Show
5	me! Great! Put the number for how much money here. If 17¢, write . . . if 73¢, write . . . All of
6	you try 35¢, now show me. No problems! Now let's learn how to write amounts more than a
7	dollar. We use 2 new marks: "$" and ".". The $ goes here, then how many dollars, then . to
8	say "and", then how many cents. Let me write a couple more then have you do it. On your
9	think pad, write $5.27; $2.98. Show me! Perfect! Now, if you have less than 10 cents when
10	writing dollar amounts, you put a 0 first. It looks like this . . . you try $3.07. Show me! Try
11	$5.01. Show me. Good. There is one more thing: if you have only dollars and no cents, write
12	00 like this . . . Try $25.00; show me. Let me mix them up now and give you practice. Hold up
13	your pad after each. $39.00; $57.89; $2.05; 35¢.
14	You are doing a great job, class.
15	
16	
17	
18	
19	
20	
21	

DISCUSSION: What did the teacher do to make this an effective lesson both in terms of classroom management and learning?

SUMMARY
INTERACTIVE TEACHING MAP

	EFFECTIVE	to less effective examples
Pretest	Pretest: brief, yields diagnostic information	Pretest: too long, doesn't yield diagnostic information
Mental Set Objective	What kids will learn, what they have to do to show they've learned, what they already know that will help, why they need to learn it	Only subject or activity mentioned: "Let's make a color wheel" or "Time for social studies"
Input	Explanation, examples of new learning, directly relevant to objective	Related but not relevant information
Modeling	Demonstration or showing visually elements of new learning (labeling critical parts)	Inadequate or poor model
Guided Practice Check For Understanding	Evidence that a majority of class can perform new skill, sample is random, occurs several times during input & at least once after input	Calling on first hand up, always calling on one child at a time, using same technique over and over, calling student just to get a right answer
Independent Practice	Kids working alone on activity related to objective, experience high success rate	Activity not related to objective, lasts too long, students lose focus, too difficult
Groups	Kids working together, not independently, teacher circulating among groups, kids are on task	Kids working alone yet sitting in groups, teacher sitting at desk, kids socializing, copying one another's work
Praise	Deserved, clearly describes behavior being reinforced, sincere	Habitual, same phrase over and over, praises child - not behavior, nonverbal doesn't match verbal
Sponge Enrichment	Short, practice activities to fill potentially wasted time, kids receive immediate feedback	Kids told to "work on anything"
Procedures Directions	Clear, step by step, written if more than two steps, checks with kids to be sure they understand, models what needs to be done, takes minimum of time	Steps not clear, mixed with additional information, many questions from kids about what to do
Reactive Management	Minor disruptions handled with minimum interruption to class, if possible - handled individually, stops behavior/disruption immediately	Overreacts to minor disruption, could be handled with less interruption to class, nagging, doesn't stop behavior
No Task Defined, # Off Task		Students finish work, nothing to do, waiting for teacher, actual number of students obviously off task

Appendix

Doug Kerr and I developed the Interactive Teaching Map for the following research project: Grant Number 79-JN-AX-0014, Supp. #1 awarded to the Center for Law and Justice, University of Washington, Seattle, by the National Institute for Juvenile Justice and Delinquency Prevention, Office of Juvenile Justice and Delinquency Prevention, U.S. Department of Justice. Joseph C. Weis is the Director and Richard L. Janvier and J. David Hawkins are Co-Directors of the project. Points of view or opinions in this book are those of the author and do not necessarily represent official position or policies of the U.S. Department of Justice.

(A special note of thanks to the following for help on the Map: Carol Barber, William Donnelly, J. David Hawkins & David Sumi.)

REFERENCES

Anderson, L. *Trade-offs in American Education: Perspectives on mastery-based instructional programs.* Program presented at International Reading Association, Chicago, 1982.

Anderson, L., Evertson, C. & Emmer, E. Dimensions in classroom management derived from recent research. *Journal of Curriculum Studies,* 1980, 12(4), 343-356.

Anderson, R. & Faust, G. *Educational Psychology.* New York: Harper & Row, 1973.

Arlin, M. Teacher transitions can disrupt time flow in classrooms. *American Educational Research Journal,* 1979, 16, 42-56.

Aronson, E., Blaney, N., Stephan, C., Sikes, J.,Snapp, M. *The Jigsaw Classroom.* Beverly Hills, California: Sage, 1978.

Bar-Tal, D. Attributional analysis of achievement-related behavior. *Review of Educational Research,* 1978, 48, 259-271.

Berliner, D. Tempus Educare. In P.Peterson & H. Walberg (Eds.), *Research on Teaching.* Berkley, Ca.:McCutchan Publishing, 1979.

Blakeslee, T. *The Right Brain.* New York: Anchor Press, 1980.

Bloom, B. *Human Characteristics and School Learning.* New York:McGraw-Hill, 1976.

Bloom, B. *All Our Children Learning.* New York: McGraw-Hill, 1981.

Bogen, J.E. Some educational implications of hemispheric specialization. In M.C. Wittrock (Ed.), *The Human Brain.* Englewood Cliffs, N.J.: Prentice-Hall, 1977.

Borg, W. Time and school learning. In C. Denham & A. Lieberman (Eds.), *Time to Learn.* Washington, D.C.: National Institute of Education, 1980.

Boyer, W. Toward an ecological perspective in education: Part II. *Phi Delta Kappan,* 1974, 55, 397-399.

Brookover, W., Beady, C., Flood, P., Schweitzer, J., & Wisenbaker, J. *School Social Systems and Student Achievement.* New York: Praeger Publishers, 1979.

Brophy, J. Teacher behavior and its effects. *Journal of Educational Psychology,*1979, 71, 733-750.

Brophy, J. Teacher praise: A functional analysis. *Review of Educational Research,* 1981, 51, 5-32.

Brophy, J. & Evertson, C. *Learning from Teaching: A Developmental Perspective.* Boston: Allyn & Bacon, 1976.

Brophy, J. & Putnam, J. Classroom management in the elementary grades. In D. Duke (Ed.) *Classroom Management: The 78th Yearbook of the National Society for the Study of Education.* Chicago: University of Chicago Press, 1979.

Carsetti, J. Motivational Activities for Reluctant Readers. Silver Spring, Maryland: Read, 1979.

Cooper, H. Pygmalion grows up: a model for teacher expectation. Communication and performance influence. *Review of Educational Research,* 1979, 49 (3), 389-410.

Coppedge, W. What the world is coming to. In H. Sobel & A. Salz (Eds.) *The Radical Papers: Readings in Education.* New York: Harper & Row, 1972.

Cornbleth, C., Davis, O., & Button, C. Expectations for pupil achievement and teacher-pupil interaction. *Social Education,* 1974, 38 (1), 54-58.

Corno, L. Classroom instruction and the matter of time. In D. Duke (Ed.) *Classroom Management, The 78th Yearbook of the National Society for the Study of Education.* Chicago: University of Chicago Press, 1979.

Cummings, C., Nelson, C., & Shaw, D. *Teaching Makes a Difference,* Teaching Inc., Edmonds, WA, 1980.

Dunn, R. & Dunn, K. *Teaching Students Through Their Individual Learning Styles: A Practical Approach.* Reston, Virginia: Reston Publishing, 1978.

Emmer, E. & Evertson, C. Effective management at the beginning of the school year in junior high classes. R & D Center for Teacher Education, The University of Texas at Austin, 1980.

Emmer, E. & Evertson, C. Synthesis of research on classroom management. *Educational Research,* 1981, 38(4), 342-347.

Epstein, H. Growth spurts during brain development: implications for educational policy and practice. In J. Chall & A. Mirsky (Eds.) *Education and the Brain.* Chicago: University of Chicago Press, 1978.

Evertson, C. Differences in instructional activities in high and low achieving junior high classes. R & D Center for Teacher Education, The University of Texas at Austin, 1980.

Evertson, C. & Anderson, L. Beginning school. *Educational Horizons,* 1979, 57, 164-168.

Fox, P. Reading as a whole brain function. *The Reading Teacher,* 1979, 33, 7-14.

Galyean, B. The application of brain-mind research to learning and curriculum development. Presentation to 1981 I/D/E/A/ Fellows Program, 1981.

Gage, N. *The Scientific Basis of the Art of Teaching.* New York: Teachers College Press, 1978.

Gansneder, B., Caldwell, M., Morris, J., Napier, J., & Bowen, L. An analysis of the association between teachers' classroom objectives and activities, *The Journal of Educational Research,* 1977, 70, 170-179.

Gazzaniga, M. Review of the split brain. In M.C. Wittrock (Ed.), *The Human Brain.* Englewood Cliffs, N.J.: Prentice-Hall, 1977.

Good, T. Teacher effectiveness in the elementary school:what we know about it now. *Journal of Teacher Education,* 1979, 30, 52-64.

Good, T. & Brophy, J. Changing teacher and student behavior: an empirical investigation. *Journal of Educational Psychology,* 1974, 66 (3), 390-405.

Good, T. & Brophy, J. *Looking in Classrooms (Second edition).* New York: Harper and Row, 1978.

Goodlad, J. Improving schooling in the 1980s: Toward the non-replication of non-events. *Educational Leadership,* 1983, 40(7), 4-7.

Higbee, K. *Your Memory—How It Works and How to Improve It.* Englewood Cliffs, N.J.: Prentice-Hall, 1977.

Hunter, M. *R X Improved Instruction.* El Segundo, Ca.: TIP Publications, 1976.

Jackson, P. *Life in Classrooms,* New York: Holt, Rinehart & Winston, 1968.

Johnson, M. & Brooks, H. Conceptualizing classroom management. In D. Duke (Ed.) *Classroom Management: The 78th Yearbook of the National Society for the Study of Education.* Chicago: University of Chicago Press, 1979.

Johnson, D., Johnson, R., & Scott, L. The effects of cooperative and individualized instruction of student attitudes and achievement. *Journal of Social Psychology,* 1978, 104, 207-216.

Kagan, S. Cooperation-competition, culture, and structural bias in classrooms. In S. Sharan, P. Hare, C. Webb, & R. Hertz-Lazarowitz (Eds.) *Cooperation in Education.* Provo, Utah: Brigham Young University Press, 1980.

Kounin, J. *Discipline and Group Management in Classrooms.* New York: Holt, Rinehart, & Winston, 1970.

Krathwohl, D., Bloom, B., & Masia, B. *Taxonomy of Educational Objectives. Handbook II: Affective Domain.* New York: David McKay Company, 1964.

Lawrence, G. Do programs reflect what research says about physical development? *Middle School Journal,* 1980, 11(2), 12-14.

Lepper, M. & Greene, D. (Eds.) *The Hidden Costs of Reward: New Perspectives on the Psychology of Human Motivation.* Hillsdale, New Jersey: Erlbaum, 1978.

Levy, J. Research synthesis on right and left hemispheres. We think with both sides of the brain. *Educational Leadership,* 1983, 40(4), 66-71.

Little, J. *School Success and Staff Development: The Role of Staff Development in Urban Desegregated Schools.* Boulder, Colorado: Center for Action Research, 1981.

Mackenzie, A. & White, R., Fieldwork in geography and longterm memory structures. *American Educational Research Journal,* 1982, 19 (4), 623-632.

MacLean, P. A mind of three minds: educating the triune brain. In J. Chall & A. Mirsky (Eds.) *Education and the Brain: The 77th Yearbook of The National Society for the Study of Education.* Chicago: University of Chicago Press, 1978.

Maehr, M. Sociocultural origins of achievement motivation. In D. Bar-Tal (Ed.) *Social Psychology of Education.* New York: John Wiley & Sons, 1978.

Mager, R. *Developing Attitude Toward Learning.* Belmont, Ca.: Fearon Publishing, 1968.

Moskowitz, G. & Hayman, J. Success strategies of inner-city teachers: a year long study. *Journal of Educational Research,* 1976, 69, 283-289.

Multi-Lingual Assessment Project. *Culturally Democratic Learning Environments.* Riverside, Ca.: Systems and Evaluations in Education, 1972.

National Council of Teachers of Mathematics, *An Agenda for Action (Recommendations for school mathematics of the 1980s).* The National Council of Teachers of Mathematics,Inc., 1980.

Popham, W. & Baker, E. *Classroom Instructional Tactics.* Englewood Cliffs, N.J.: Prentice-Hall, 1973.

Postman, N. The politics of reading. In H. Sobel A. Salz (Eds.) *The Radical Papers.* New York: Harper & Row, 1972.

Postman, N. & Weingartner, C. *Teaching as a Subversive Activity.* New York: Dell Pub. Co., Inc., 1969.

Prichard, A. & Taylor, J. *Accelerating Learning.* Novato, Ca.: Academic Therapy Publications, 1980.

Purkey, W. *Inviting School Success.* Belmont, Ca.: Wadsworth Publishing, 1978.

Quigley, C. Needed: A revolution in thinking. *NEA Journal,* 1968, 57, 8-10+.

Raina, M. Education of the left and the right. *International Review of Education,* 1979, 25(1), 8-19.

Rosenshine, B. Content, time, and direct instruction. In P. Peterson & H. Walberg (Eds.), *Research on Teaching.* Berkley, Ca.: McCutchan Publishing, 1979.

Rosenshine, B. How time is spent in elementary classrooms. In C. Denham & A. Lieberman (Eds.) *Time to Learn.* Washington, D.C.: National Institute of Education, 1980.

Rowe, M. *Teaching Science as Continuous Inquiry.* New York: McGraw Hill, 1978.

Rutter, M., Maughan, B., Mortimore, P., Ouston, J., & Smith, A. *Fifteen Thousand Hours: Secondary Schools and Their Effects on Children.* Cambridge: Harvard University Press, 1979.

Sanford, J. & Evertson, C. Beginning the school year at a low SES junior high. Austin, Texas: Research and Development Center for Teacher Education, 1980.

Scribner, H. What needs reforming? In H. Sobel & A. Salz (Eds.) *The Radical Papers.* New York: Harper & Row, 1972.

Shane, H. Looking to the future: reassessment of educational issues of the 1970s. *Phi Delta Kappan,* 1973, 54(5), 326-337.

Shoemaker, J. & Fraser, H. What principals can do: some implications from studies of effective schooling. *Phi Delta Kappan,* 1981, 63, 178-182.

Slavin, R. Student team learning. In S. Sharan, P. Hare, C. Webb, & R. Herz-Lazarowitz (Eds.) *Cooperation in Education.* Provo, Utah: Brigham Young University Press, 1980.

Spillman, C. Classroom management: mystery or mastery? *Education,* 1980, 101(1), 41-45.

Springer, S. & Deutsch, G. *Left Brain, Right Brain.* San Francisco: W.H. Freeman & Co., 1981.

Stallings, J. Allocated academic learning time revisited, or beyond time on task. *Educational Researcher,* 1980, 9 (11), 11-16.

Stodolsky, S. & Lesser, G. Learning patterns in the disadvantaged. *Harvard Educational Review,* 1967, 37, 546-593.

Tikunoff, W., Berliner, D., & Rist, R. Abstract from Special Study: An Ethnographic Study of the Forty Classrooms of the Beginning Teacher Evaluation Study Known Sample. San Francisco: Far West Laboratory, 1975.

Tryon, G. The measurement and treatment of test anxiety. *Review of Educational Research,* 1980, 50, 343-372.

Vasquez, J. Locus of control, social class, and learning. Los Angeles, Ca.:National Dissemination & Assessment Center (Paper Series), 1978.

Vitale, B. More on a right-brained approach to learning. *Early Years,* 1982, 13(3), 42-43.

Ware, B. What rewards do students want. *Phi Delta Kappan.* 1978, 59, 352-355.

Weingartner, C. Communication, education & change. In H. Sobel & A. Salz (Eds.) *The Radical Papers.* New York: Harper & Row, 1972.

Witkin, H., Moore, G., Goodenough, D. & Cox. P. Field-dependent and field-independent cognitive styles and their educational implications. *Review of Educational Research,* 1977, 47, 1-64.

Wittrock, M. The generative process of memory. In M. Wittrock (Ed.), *The Human Brain.* Englewood Cliffs, N.J.: Prentice-Hall, 1977.

Worsham, M. & Evertson, C. Systems of student accountability for written work in junior high English classes. R & D Center for Teacher Education, The University of Texas at Austin, 1980.